Penguin Critical Studies

Middlemarch

Catherine Neale was educated at Newnham College, Cambridge, and at the University of Edinburgh. She has taught at the Open University, the University of Edinburgh and the Extra-Mural Department of the University of Birmingham. She is currently Senior Lecturer in English at Worcester College of Higher Education. She has also written, with Roger Ebbatson, a critical study of *A Passage to India* for Penguin Books.

Penguin Critical Studies
Joint Advisory Editors:
Stephen Coote and Bryan Loughrey

George Eliot

Middlemarch

Catherine Neale

Penguin Books

PENGUIN BOOKS

Published by the Penguin Group
27 Wrights Lane, London W8 5TZ, England
Viking Penguin Inc., 40 West 23rd Street, New York, New York 10010, USA
Penguin Books Australia Ltd, Ringwood, Victoria, Australia
Penguin Books Canada Ltd, 2801 John Street, Markham, Ontario, Canada L3R 1B4
Penguin Books (NZ) Ltd, 182–190 Wairau Road, Auckland 10, New Zealand

Penguin Books Ltd, Registered Offices: Harmondsworth, Middlesex, England

First published 1989

Copyright © Catherine Neale, 1989
All rights reserved

Made and printed in Great Britain by
Richard Clay Ltd, Bungay, Suffolk
Filmset in Monophoto Times

Contents

Introductory Note

Middlemarch is a novel about a young woman who decides, against the advice of her friends, to marry an elderly scholar. It is about a doctor who arrives in a small provincial town at the beginning of his career. It is about a fictional town called Middlemarch in the years 1829 to 1832. It is about a provincial young lady called Rosamond and a middle-aged banker called Bulstrode. It is about heroism, martyrdom, egoism, failure, marriage, vocation, history, science, knowledge ... Because of its scale and range of subject, no one reader can go away with the whole story. I have chosen to divide this critical study of *Middlemarch* into three main sections. The first provides information about the author, the novel, and the times: background information, therefore, that helps the reader to place *Middlemarch*. The second section suggests a number of contexts within which to read the novel, together with a number of perspectives within which to understand certain features of the novel. Those readings and understandings appear, at times, contradictory, since they are derived from a number of different critical positions. In the third section, closer analysis throws up a series of interpretations, although, once again, they overlap and do not necessarily cohere. By providing a series of versions of *Middlemarch*, I hope to explore with the reader the seriousness, and the excitement, of this important text – without offering any final answers.

The text which is used throughout this study, and from which page references are taken, is the Penguin edition edited by W. J. Harvey, published in 1965. A select bibliography is included at the end. Quotations from books given there are not referenced in the text. Occasional quotations from other critics are noted when they appear.

I should like to record my thanks to the Librarian and staff of the library of Worcester College of Higher Education. I am most grateful to the following friends and colleagues for their advice and encouragement: Roger Ebbatson, C. W. Kemp, Dilwyn Porter, Rick Rylance, Ian Small and Ted Townley.

I Biographical and Historical Background

1. The Life of George Eliot

Mary Anne Evans, who was also to be known in the course of her lifetime as Marian Evans, Marian Lewes, George Eliot and Marian Cross, was born in 1819 at South Farm, Arbury, in Warwickshire. Her father, Robert Evans, was agent to Francis Parker Newdigate of Arbury Hall. She was the youngest surviving child of his second marriage, and was deeply attached to her brother Isaac, born in 1816. Although Mary Anne Evans was to travel widely, both intellectually and geographically, from her birthplace, she shows in her work a continual awareness of the memories, the family bonds and rural scenes, of her childhood. In *The Mill on the Floss*, she depicts a relationship between brother and sister that reflects much of the emotion of her own experience, while several of her novels are set in the Midlands. While writing *Middlemarch*, in 1869, she composed eleven sonnets with the title of 'Brother and Sister', and in *Middlemarch* she describes a brother and sister, Fred and Rosamond Vincy, travelling leisurely through the Midlands countryside:

Little details gave each field a particular physiognomy, dear to the eyes that have looked on them from childhood: the pool in the corner where the grasses were dank and trees leaned whisperingly; the great oak shadowing a bare place in mid-pasture; the high bank where the ash-trees grew; the sudden slope of the old marl-pit making a red background for the burdock; the huddled roofs and ricks of the homestead without a traceable way of approach; the grey gate and fences against the depths of the bordering wood; and the stray hovel, its old, old thatch full of mossy hills and valleys with wondrous modulations of light and shadow such as we travel far to see in later life, and see larger, but not more beautiful. These are the things that make the gamut of joy in landscape to midland-bred souls – the things they toddled among, or perhaps learned by heart standing between their father's knees while he drove leisurely. (p. 131)

The Vincy section of the novel was one of the first to be conceived; Fred Vincy's attachment to Mary Garth is significantly an attachment based on childhood memories, while in the character of Caleb Garth, with his reverence for 'business', we may detect a portrait of Mary Anne's father, Robert Evans.

Mary Anne was educated at girls' boarding schools in the Midlands, including Mrs Wallington's Boarding School in Nuneaton and the Miss

Franklins' School in Coventry, where the curriculum was fairly conventional for girls at the time: music, drawing, English, French, history and arithmetic. From her schooldays Mary Anne developed a strong commitment to Evangelicalism, an earnest and self-denying form of religion, which tended to be the norm among Protestants at that time. Her adolescent years were marked by an inclination towards renunciation and asceticism. After her mother's death in 1836, she returned to live with her father at Griff Farm, but continued an extensive reading programme, mainly on religious topics, and studied Italian, Latin and German. Indeed, she remained a voracious and serious reader throughout her life. When her brother married in 1841, she and her father moved to Coventry, and here she met a young couple, Charles and Caroline Bray.

Any summary of George Eliot's life is inevitably bound up with the currents of the time. Charles Bray, having been a committed Evangelical, had turned from religion to the 'science' of phrenology, the reading of character from physiological characteristics. Caroline's brother, Charles Hennell, had published *An Inquiry into the Origins of Christianity* in 1838, in which he submitted the Gospels to textual criticism – querying the dates of their composition and testing the historical circumstances that might have caused them to be written. He deduced that they were written about two generations after the events and that they drew on myth and legend. His general conclusion was that though Christianity could not be accepted as divine revelation, it was certainly 'the purest form yet existing of natural religion'.

Mary Anne had already been turning her attention from the sternness of Evangelicalism to contemporary investigations into divine and biblical authority, a flourishing field of study particularly in Germany. She was also becoming more interested in the pleasures of secular literature. Her meeting with the Brays and the Hennells consolidated this trend away from Evangelicalism in her thinking, and in January 1842 she announced to her father that she could no longer accompany him to church. Her family and friends tried to convince her of her error, but as one acquaintance, a Baptist minister, said, 'That young lady must have had the devil at her elbow to suggest her doubts, for there was not a book that I recommended to her in support of Christian evidences that she had not read.' In a letter to her father, she wrote, 'I regard [the scriptures] as histories consisting of mingled truth and fiction ... I could not without vile hypocrisy and a miserable truckling to the smile of the world for the sake of my supposed interests, profess to join in worship which I wholly disapprove.'[1] Eventually, however, in the face of her father's outrage and distress, she agreed to attend church with him, but retained the right to her new opinions. This significant and far-reaching episode demonstrates her willingness to act publicly and sincerely on deeply held convictions.

From 1842 until her father's death in 1849, Mary Anne enjoyed a close friendship with the Brays and with Sara Hennell, Caroline Bray's sister. This friendship opened up for her a new circle of acquaintances in the intellectual world. In 1843 she spent some weeks with the elderly Dr Brabant at Devizes: Dr Brabant pursued interests in theological science, and Mary Anne was to be his intellectual companion-cum-secretary. A mild flirtation was stopped by Mrs Brabant, and Mary Anne returned hastily to Coventry. Dr Brabant is sometimes canvassed as the original for Casaubon in *Middlemarch*. In 1844 she took over from her friend Rufa Brabant, who was marrying Charles Hennell, the translation from the German of *Das Leben Jesu* by Strauss: *The Life of Jesus, Critically Examined*. This was an investigation into, and secular-ization of, the biblical version of Jesus's life, first published in Germany in 1835. Strauss's biography removes the messianic claims implicit in the Gospels; miracles are, according to Strauss, imaginative symbols of states of feeling. Mary Anne's translation was published in 1846. Gordon Haight, one of her biographers, says that 'Few books of the nineteenth century have had a profounder influence on religious thought in England': the corrosive effects of German biblical criticism first reached a wide audience in England through this translation.

The Brays took Mary Anne abroad for a holiday after her father's funeral, and when they returned, she remained in Geneva where she spent eight months. Ten years later she described her state of mind at the time: 'When I was at Geneva I had not yet lost the attitude of antagonism which belongs to the renunciation of *any* belief – also I was very unhappy and in a state of discord and rebellion towards my own lot.'[2] At the age of thirty, she was relatively plain, solitary and lonely, and seeking some direction in her life; but she was also very ac-complished. The continental visit enabled her to make the decision to live and work as a journalist in London when she returned to England. Her father had left her sufficient money to accord her a basic income on which to make the experiment. In January 1851 she took rooms in the house of John Chapman.

John Chapman, who ran a publishing and bookselling business from his house in the Strand, conducted a *ménage à trois* with his wife and the children's governess. Marian, as she now called herself, was soon the object of both women's jealousy, and was forced to return to

Coventry. But her intellectual powers were necessary to Chapman when he took over the editorship of *The Westminster Review*, and she shortly returned. In 1852, the first edition of the new *Westminster Review* appeared. An anonymous co-editing and journalistic role was to occupy Marian for the next two years. The highly regarded radical periodical covered politics, history, reform, philosophy, science, religion and literature, and Marian made substantial contributions to it.

In 1852, Marian suffered yet another disappointment in her emotional life. She became friendly with Herbert Spencer, the philosopher and psychologist, who wrote that he admired 'the greatness of her intellect conjoined with her womanly qualities'. But he was chary of returning her affection and of meeting her need for closer companionship. However, in 1853 she was also becoming increasingly involved in a friendship with G. H. Lewes.

Gillian Beer has commented on 'the extraordinary range of extending interests that Lewes and George Eliot shared'. He was a practised and versatile journalist, and had been writing periodical articles, philosophy, biography and drama, since his youth. During the 1850s he developed a considerable and informed interest in the scientific movements of the time. It was certainly he who gave Marian the security and confidence to try writing fiction, and his support cannot be underestimated. But he was constrained by unusual domestic circumstances. He had married in 1841, and he and his wife shared liberal ideas about marriage. After four children had been born, Agnes Lewes formed a relationship with the couple's close friend, Thornton Hunt. Her fifth son's father was Hunt, but Lewes registered the child as his. This condonation of his wife's adultery was to prevent Lewes ever from divorcing her, although by the time that he and Marian became involved, he had recognized that his marriage had broken down irretrievably.

In July 1854 Marian and Lewes left for Germany together. Their departure caused shock and grave disapproval among the circle of their acquaintance and in the wider London society of which they were both a part. What was a deep commitment was almost inevitably seen by many as a reprehensible self-indulgence. During 1853 Marian had been translating Ludwig Feuerbach's *Wesen des Christentums*: 'The Essence of Christianity', first published in 1841. Her translation was published just before the departure for Germany and was the only one of her publications to carry the name Marian Evans. Feuerbach argued that the essence of Christianity is really those quintessentially *human* attributes of reason, affection, sympathy, will and love, and that religion is the manifestation of human beings' need to imagine a perfect being:

'The essence of faith is the idea that that which man wishes actually is.' He emphasized love as the great force in human lives, linking human attributes to 'divine' qualities. Sexual love, according to Feuerbach, was the essence of this:

But marriage – we mean, of course, marriage as the free bond of love – is sacred in itself, by the very nature of the union which is therein effected. That alone is a religious marriage which is a true marriage, which corresponds to the essence of marriage – of love.

'I everywhere agree,' Marian wrote to Sara Hennell in April 1854. Feuerbach's ideas give some demonstration of the nature of Marian's decision to live with Lewes without being able to marry him. It was to be a committed and sacred union. His ideas are also one of the sources of the emphasis on sympathetic love in the novels of George Eliot.

When Marian Evans and G. H. Lewes returned to England in 1855, they settled in London as Mr and Mrs Lewes. Their relationship caused few people to visit them, and Marian's life, in particular, was isolated from a wider social existence. To her profound regret, her brother broke off all communication with her when she eventually announced her 'marriage' to him. She wrote to Cara Bray:

Light and easily broken ties are what I neither desire theoretically nor could live for practically. Women who are satisfied with such ties do *not* act as I have done – they obtain what they desire and are still invited to dinner.[3]

There are tones of conviction and bitterness here, but it is evident that both the isolation, and the emotional contentment, gave Marian the opportunity for extensive reading and writing. She continued to contribute articles to *The Westminster Review*; two of her most famous essays, 'The Natural History of German Life' and 'Silly Novels by Lady Novelists' date from 1856. And in September 1856 she began to write her first piece of fiction, 'The Sad Fortunes of the Reverend Amos Barton', which was to be the opening story in *Scenes of Clerical Life*. 'Amos Barton' was initially published in two parts in *Blackwood's Magazine*.

'Whatever may be the success of my stories, I shall be resolute in preserving my incognito, having observed that a *nom de plume* secures all the advantages without the disagreeables of reputation,'[4] wrote Marian in her letter to her publisher Blackwood, announcing for the first time her chosen pseudonym, George Eliot. Among the reading public, there was intense speculation as to who the author might actually be. The adoption of a male pseudonym seems to have been caused by several pressures: contemporary reactions to women writers and her wish to be regarded in a more serious light, Marian's own innate reticence, and her anomalous status in her personal life. *Scenes of Clerical Life* (1857) was followed by *Adam Bede* (1859). There was some anxiety over the publication of *Adam Bede*, both George Eliot and Blackwood feeling that prior knowledge on the part of readers that the author was a woman, and also a notorious woman living with G. H. Lewes, would prejudice the novel's reception. Eventually, after the impressive success of *Adam Bede* with the reading public, the mystery surrounding the pseudonym was dropped.

The 1860s was a decade of creative activity and increasing recognition for George Eliot, despite a developing nervousness prior to the composition of each of her works. *The Mill on the Floss*, *Silas Marner*, *Romola*, and *Felix Holt* were all published in these years. *Middlemarch* appeared in serial parts in 1871 and 1872, and was published in one volume in 1873. Approval was unanimous, and the novel marked George Eliot's acceptance in both literary and social circles. By the time that *Daniel Deronda* was published in 1876, George Eliot was highly respected and enjoyed a reputation for wisdom, moral authority, and sympathetic understanding of the human condition.

G. H. Lewes died in November 1878. George Eliot's affliction was mitigated somewhat when, in May 1880, she married John Cross, a family friend twenty years her junior. Once again she had succeeded in surprising her friends. The marriage brought for her a longed-for reconciliation with her brother Isaac, but she died soon after, in December 1880.

Whatever one may think about the relevance or otherwise of a writer's biography to a text, George Eliot's extraordinary life demands our attention. She was unusual in so many ways: her determined rejection of religious orthodoxy, her independence in choosing to leave her family milieu and to work in London and abroad, her lifelong commitment to intellectual pursuits and radical ideas, her decision to live with a married man, and, of course, her authorship of a considerable number of profound works of fiction. This amazing biography stands behind many of the concerns of *Middlemarch*. The novel conveys an ambivalence about religion, and a complex attitude towards the notions of family life and one's place of origin. Several of the main characters are orphans, travellers or outcasts. It portrays a provincial background from which some characters have to escape to a richer cultural life elsewhere, as well as betraying a nostalgic fondness for one kind of past.

2. The Composition and Serialization of *Middlemarch*

At the end of every year, it was George Eliot's custom to assess her year's work and to note in her journal her plans for the coming year. One of her projects for 1869 was a novel called *Middlemarch*. She began to write it on or about 19 July 1869, but the novel whose title was already chosen appears at this stage to have been about Lydgate, Fred and Rosamond Vincy, Featherstone, and the Garths, and to have commenced with the scenes in Chapters 11 to 15, dealing with Lydgate, Fred's embarrassment with Featherstone, and his application to Bulstrode for confirmation that he has not borrowed on the strength of his expectations. The summer and autumn months of 1869 were difficult ones for George Eliot and G. H. Lewes: Lewes's son, Thornton, had returned home from Natal, suffering from tuberculosis of the spine. After great pain, he died on 19 October 1869. There is little information about the composition of *Middlemarch* during this period.

Over a year later, on 2 December 1870, George Eliot wrote in her journal about another fiction that she was writing:

I am experimenting in a story which I began without any very serious intention of carrying it out lengthily. It is a subject which has been recorded among my possible themes ever since I began to write fiction, but will probably take new shapes in the development. I am today at p. 44.[5]

The provisional title was 'Miss Brooke'. Between December 1870 and March 1871 she combined the two works in progress, probably because of the similarity in situation of Lydgate and Dorothea, and because both works were set in the late 1820s. By 19 March 1871 she had written the first eighteen chapters and what is now Chapter 23.

The potential scale of the novel was already becoming apparent, and she noted to herself, 'My present fear is that I have too much matter, too many *momentii*.' Shortly afterwards, G. H. Lewes suggested to Blackwood, the publisher, a form of serialization which would be helpful in the composition and would also be financially beneficial: eight half-volume parts would be published bi-monthly, producing a four-volume book instead of the usual 'three-decker'. Having reached agreement with Blackwood about the form of publication, and with the problems of combining two disparate stories behind her, George Eliot

9

settled down to writing. By August 1871 she was composing Book III, finishing it on 29 October. Book IV was well in progress by Christmas 1871 and, despite the Lewes's lively social programme, Book V was sent to Blackwood in May 1872. Book VI was completed by 2 July, Book VII by 7 August, and Book VIII in September 1872. She confessed to a correspondent that the last year had been 'a sort of nightmare in which I have been scrambling on the slippery bank of a pool, just keeping my head above water'.[6]

Inevitably, the length and complexity of the novel necessitated research and planning, and two 'Quarries' exist, showing George Eliot's investigations into political dates, medical research, and scholarship, as well as meticulous planning of plot and overall structure. The combining of the first *Middlemarch* with 'Miss Brooke' entailed detailed revision and the character of Rosamond underwent some modification at that point of the writing: her complacency, determination and vanity were relatively late additions. Many critics have commented on the apparent identification of George Eliot with Dorothea, some maintaining that over-identification leads to a misjudgement in characterization and portrayal, but it is tantalizing to learn that when asked about the inspiration for Casaubon, George Eliot, 'with humorous solemnity, which was quite in earnest nevertheless, pointed to her own heart'. Whether she meant that Casaubon was drawn from certain traits of character that she recognized in herself, or, alternatively, that he represents someone once dear to her, remains unclear.

The sheer ambition and panoramic spread of *Middlemarch* were present from early in the writing. In July 1871 she wrote to Blackwood,

I don't see how I can leave anything out, because I hope there is nothing that will be seen to be irrelevant to my design, which is to show the gradual action of ordinary causes rather than exceptional, and to show this in some directions which have not been from time immemorial the beaten path.[7]

And although she distrusted serialization, feeling that her fiction was not best represented in short sections, the form of publication devised by Lewes (which was not the conventional scheme of serialization) produced unity within each Book and possibly a greater overall structure: from Book III onwards, all the stories are present in each half-volume. As Lewes had said, in suggesting the format, 'Each part would have a certain unity and completeness in itself with separate title'.

Publication began on 1 December 1871 and, with monthly instead of bi-monthly issues of the last three Books, was completed in December

1872. Tremendous rapport developed between the author and her readers. Commercially, *Middlemarch* was a success: the bi-monthly parts selling at five shillings apiece, sold nearly 5,000 copies each. A four-volume edition in 1873, costing one guinea, sold a further 3,000 copies, and in 1874, a one-volume reprint at 7s. 6d. sold 13,000 copies in six months. By 1879, *Middlemarch* had brought George Eliot about £9,000. Reviews were almost universally admiring, the key-note being that *Middlemarch* was George Eliot's masterpiece.

3. George Eliot and Currents of the Time

Every work of literature has vital links to the time in which it was written, and as readers, we may, as a general rule, advert to this 'historical context' to 'use' it for help in interpreting references, vocabulary and cultural assumptions. This procedure, however, creates a system of relatively simple oppositions between text and context, literature and background, the aim being explanation. Yet George Eliot's novels invite a more sustained and urgent attention to the many intellectual developments and controversies of the nineteenth century on the part of the reader. Because of her experiences as an intellectual and as a woman, and because of the particular concerns of *Middlemarch*, the currents of the time come into a complex interrelationship with the fiction that was produced. *Middlemarch* not only mirrors contemporary debates, it participates in them.

George Eliot is often cited as a representative of a major trend in Victorian thought, though paradoxically she is representative because she is unique: as Ioan Williams says, 'Among the major novelists of the first two thirds of the century she alone had gone through the religious crisis we often think of as typically Victorian.'[8] Her repudiation for herself of formal religion was caused by her reading in the most advanced areas of investigation during the 1840s and 1850s, and her subsequent development of a personal philosophy consistently reveals a sustained commitment to the implications of current thought. As late as 1874, she wrote to a correspondent: 'the idea of God, so far as it has been a high spiritual influence, is the ideal of a goodness entirely human (i.e. an exaltation of the human)'.

Critical investigation of George Eliot's personal philosophy sometimes meets the charge that such concentration detracts from the artistic integrity of her work. However, a novel such as *Middlemarch* presents itself as an active contribution to nineteenth-century ideas. Three brief passages from the text may help to make the point:

any one watching keenly the stealthy convergence of human lots, sees a slow preparation of effects from one life on another, which tells like a calculated irony on the indifference or the frozen stare with which we look at our unintroduced neighbour. (p. 122)

Circumstances were almost sure to be on the side of Rosamond's idea, which had a shaping activity and looked through watchful blue eyes, whereas Lydgate's lay blind and unconcerned as a jelly-fish which gets melted without knowing it. (p. 305)

Mr Hawley's disgust at the notion of the *Pioneer* being edited by an emissary, and of Brooke becoming actively political – as if a tortoise of desultory pursuits should protrude its small head ambitiously and become rampant . . . (p. 394)

Why does the author's language in the first example emphasize stealthiness, slow effects and irony? Why are Rosamond and Lydgate described so carefully as if they were in some predatory conflict to do with marine animals? Why (although it is so funny and apt, perhaps) is Mr Brooke linked with the simile of a tortoise acting out of character? Taken together, these passages illustrate how the authorial practice, the themes and the imagery of *Middlemarch* all participate in methodology and language prevalent in the mid nineteenth century.

In order to explain the ideas underlying these passages from *Middlemarch*, it is necessary to sketch in the intellectual climates in which George Eliot and *Middlemarch* are situated, in particular those scientific and philosophical debates that permeate her thoughts and her fiction. Subsequent sections will consider some of the contexts – historical, religious, formal and literary – that can aid the reader of *Middlemarch*.

It appears that, in general, nineteenth-century thought moved with increasing momentum towards a version of the world that stressed gradual development, change and growth, and that the methodology used was scientific, inquiring and sceptical. Similar trends occurred within a startlingly short number of years in the supposedly unrelated fields of population theory, biblical criticism, geology, psychology and anthropology. German historical methodology was adopting the criterion of a rigorous, quasi-scientific examination of available evidence, for example, as can be perceived in Strauss's *Das Leben Jesu*, which George Eliot translated. In the field of geology, Charles Lyell's *Principles of Geology*, published in three volumes during the years 1830 to 1833, was widely read. Lyell demonstrated that geological change proceeds in a gradual and orderly manner. This was in direct contradiction to popular and literal readings of the Bible on the topic of geology, where the occasion of the Flood in Genesis, for example, afforded adherents 'proof' that change occurs through divine intervention and the imposition of catastrophe. Geology was a discipline which provided perhaps the most visible signs of historical development in the field of science, and Lyell himself was reluctant to pursue his research into more 'nebulous' areas. He argued that natural causes were evident in geology, but in Volume II of *Principles of Geology* he rejected natural causes, and therefore evolution, as an explanation of human life. However, the first volume of Lyell's *Principles* was a major item of the young Charles Darwin's luggage when he embarked on his formative voyage in the *Beagle* at the end of 1831, and the later volumes were sent out to him during his trip.

The arguments of Thomas Malthus in *An Essay on the Principle of Population* in 1798 had cast doubts on a divine or beneficent plan for humanity. Malthus reasoned that population increases in successive generations by geometric progression while food supplies only increase by arithmetic progression. Unless human beings restrained their sexual appetites, he suggested, the only inevitable influences which would constrain population, and therefore balance food with people, were disasters such as war, famine, plague and vice. The theories of David Ricardo, in particular his treatise *On the Principles of Political Economy and Taxation* (1817), tended to endorse this harsh scenario. Malthus's ideas were later to strike Charles Darwin as a natural law about human life, and they certainly added weight to his arguments regarding plants and animals in *The Origin of Species* (1859).

The *Beagle* was despatched by the Admiralty on a long voyage round the world, with the aims of continuing the charting of the South American coast, and of making a more accurate 'plan' of longitude. Darwin was appointed unpaid naturalist on the voyage. It was to prove an experience from which much of his later work drew its practical basis. At Punta Alta on the east coast of South America, Darwin made the first of many discoveries of fossils – the skeleton of the extinct species, Megatherium, or giant sloth. It led him to question the previously received notion of the fixity and permanence of species, for here was an example of an extinct species. Moreover, the fossil bones were embedded in marine shells that could still, in the nineteenth century, be found on beaches: the significance of this was that there could have been no 'catastrophe' to extinguish Megatherium because in that case the marine shells would also have been swept out of existence. Later in the trip, Darwin found fossil seashells at a height of 12,000 ft in the Andes, a discovery that implied that at some earlier geological period the Andes had been submerged under the sea, and had subsequently risen to form a mountain range on dry land. Thus, geological formations were continuously shifting and changing. On the Galapagos Islands he encountered the giant tortoises and giant lizards (iguanas, as we now know them) which, together with a multitude of other animal and plant forms, provided a laboratory-like specimen of unique species, varying gradually between islands in the archipelago depending on distance, and according to differing environments. This provided Darwin with observations on the adaptation of species to their environment.

It took Darwin more than twenty years to formulate his ideas fully, in the extensive work, the *Origin of Species*, published in 1859. Previously, plants had been classified by their reproductive organs according to a system devised by the eighteenth-century Swedish botanist, Carl Linnaeus. Linnaeus introduced a notion of order, and more precisely, a definition of genera and species, into natural science, that was widely accepted and that had the effect of emphasizing aspects of natural history to do with categorization and fixity. Ironically, perhaps, it was at meetings of the Linnaean Society, founded in 1788, that Darwin's hypotheses were first set forth in 1858. Darwin argued, from close study of plants and animals, that species change and adapt according to their environment. However, just as some members of a species expire because they lack, say, appropriate protective colouring, or fail to mate because they fail to attract a mate in competition, so whole species may become extinct if the environment alters sufficiently to make them ill-equipped for survival. In the struggle for survival, the 'fittest' survive: those fitted best by virtue of protective colouring, inherited from previous 'generations' and consequently passed on when they successfully mate. Therefore, a species constantly evolves in favour of the fittest members of that species, and variations in species occur according to geographical or temporal variations in the environment.

Darwin was not alone in his slow but relentless progress towards these conclusions. Interest in physical and biological life was matched by attempts to analyse in scientific ways the workings of the mind. Evolutionary theory, psychology and anthropology were all moving in similar directions at this time. The 'science' of phrenology, so popular in the 1830s and 1840s, and in which Charles Bray had been so interested, was an early example of a shift towards 'scientific' investigations of phenomena. Phrenologists assumed that mental qualities reside within the brain, and that areas denoting certain qualities, or the subject's lack of certain qualities, could be identified by irregularities, bumps or depressions on the exterior of the skull. It was, therefore, a practice that claimed to define personality from the physical shape of the skull. This rather literal analysis of the relationship between psychology and physiology was to be taken up in the 1860s again by Spencer, Huxley and Lewes, using the insights offered in Darwin's work. In 1852, Herbert Spencer had anticipated some of Darwin's ideas in an article in *The Leader* entitled 'The Development Hypothesis', and he followed this up in 1862 with *First Principles*. Later, he came increasingly to debate laws of evolution in the wider arena of human as well as plant and animal development. Darwin's own work was nearly pre-empted by parallel, and uncannily similar, ideas developed in the late 1850s by a scientist living in the Far East, Alfred Russell Wallace. These ideas, then, were occurring to many individuals at roughly the same time.

But Darwin drew the fire of opponents most clearly, possibly because of the sheer length, thoroughness, and authority of his exposition. In fact, the effect of all the parallel investigations in seemingly disparate areas was focused in reactions to the *Origin of Species*. While many readers accepted the logic of Darwin's arguments, many others reacted violently to the implicit reordering of assumptions about religion and ethics. The evolutionary world was perceived as predatory and potentially violent in its struggles for survival, and therefore questions of the existence of a benevolent God, of the biblical version of the creation of the first human being, of necessity and free will, matter and spirit, were all raised by, and implicated in, the Darwinian hypothesis. In various public controversies in the early 1860s, Darwin was ably defended by Thomas Huxley. The most famous occasion was at a meeting of the British Association in Oxford in June 1860, when Bishop Wilberforce, before an audience of 700 people, sneeringly asked Huxley, whether 'it was through his grandfather or his grandmother that he claimed his descent from a monkey'. Huxley concluded his reply by saying that he would not be ashamed to have a monkey for his ancestor, but that he would be 'ashamed to be connected with a man who used great gifts to obscure the truth'. In the ensuing pandemonium, one lady even fainted.

Returning to those three passages from *Middlemarch*, it becomes clear that when Mr Brooke is likened to a tortoise, the simile is not fortuitous. Just as Mr Brooke's behaviour in becoming 'actively political' is startling and unlikely, so it is impossible to imagine a tortoise suddenly becoming 'rampant'. A tortoise would risk its survival by behaving in such a way. It is changing its characteristic behaviour suddenly and for no apparent reason. Being a 'tortoise', it is not Mr Brooke's function to be aggressive or outspoken. Consequently, this tiny parenthesis indicates how Mr Brooke risks his 'survival', and how he is out of touch with his environment, Middlemarch.

The way in which Rosamond schemes and observes 'through watchful blue eyes' like a creature about to attack, while Lydgate, like a jelly-fish, is her unsuspecting prey, conveys a Darwinian picture of struggle between two species within an environment. They are, it is suggested, locked into the roles of predator and victim. Lydgate, like the jelly-fish, will be 'melted', and perhaps he, like some species, will eventually become an extinct type.

When the author refers to 'the stealthy convergence of human lots', there is a reference to geological theories of the slow, inexorable, and almost unnoticeable movement of land-masses. In talking about 'a calculated irony', though, George Eliot hints at the tensions between a description of the world in evolutionary terms, and a view of the world in which events are directed by a divine consciousness. To human beings who believe in God, such 'convergence' of human lives appears to be 'calculated', but also ironic.

The novel bears witness to contemporaneous advances in several disciplines, but George Eliot, like many thoughtful Victorians, felt compelled to confront certain questions, and to pursue lines of thought that might offer solutions. What were the implications for human beings in a chain of evolution? Do human beings differ from animals, and if so, how? Without God, what happens to morality? Disraeli, for example, in a speech at Oxford in 1864, asked, 'Is man an ape or an angel?' and answered with conviction, 'My Lord, I am on the side of the angels.' George Eliot's initial reaction may be seen in a letter to Barbara Bodichon, written in December 1859:

We have been reading Darwin's Book on the 'Origin of Species' just now: it makes an epoch, as the expression of his thorough adhesion, after long years of study, to the Doctrine of Development ... it will have a great effect in the scientific world, causing a thorough and open discussion of a question about which people have hitherto felt timid. So the world gets on step by step towards brave clearness and honesty! But to me the Development theory and all other explanations of processes by which things came to be, produce a feeble impression compared with the mystery that lies under the processes.[9]

George Eliot enjoyed the close personal friendships of Spencer and Lewes; she was visited by the physicist Tyndall and by Clifford, the mathematician; she was accustomed to review recent advanced thought for *The Westminster Review*. Testing and assimilating at every step, she traced for herself an alternative and conscientious philosophy that is in many ways representative of Victorian thought, but is in some ways highly idiosyncratic. Basil Willey describes her path in the following way:

Probably no English writer of the time, and certainly no novelist, more fully epitomizes the century; her development is a paradigm, her intellectual biography a graph, of its most decided trend. Starting from evangelical Christianity, the curve passes through doubt to a reinterpreted Christ and a religion of humanity: beginning with God, it ends in Duty.

Her translation of Ludwig Feuerbach's *Essence of Christianity* provided her with a reading of human nature that emphasized emotion, goodness and affection. Feuerbach argued that human beings create God in perceiving a goodness within humanity generally, and in that perception also see a way of rising above lower individual human qualities of egoism and subjectivity. He therefore shifted the focus of attention from God to human beings, and in stressing emotion, showed humanity as possessed of the potential for 'holiness' from within. For example, 'God suffers' means 'it is divine to suffer for others'; the Resurrection embodies a human desire for a certainty of immortality. Feuerbach went on to say that the individual achieves his or her human (and therefore divine) potential by learning the comparative insignificance of his or her ego, and then, through the suffering that this lesson causes, develops sympathy with others. Finally, he or she attains a selfless but fulfilling identification with 'humanity' or with others – this, according to Feuerbach, in fact, allows the 'divine' within the human to blossom. Feuerbach's philosophy enacts a faith in development and progress that can be found everywhere in Victorian thought. It also, significantly, stresses suffering, submission and sacrifice as the gateways to meaningful existence.

In the late 1850s, George Eliot undertook a translation from the Latin of the *Theological-Political Treatise* by the seventeenth-century Dutch philosopher, Spinoza. Despite circumstances that caused the translation never to be published, Spinozan ideas quite evidently helped George Eliot to consolidate the ideas she found in Feuerbach. Spinoza, working on a definition of human nature as dominated by the emotions, argued that by the exercise of the strong emotion of not wishing to incur evil, human beings can achieve moral sympathy and existence in the social sphere. Thus, he reasoned, even though human beings are ruled by passion and self-interest, these can themselves channel moral behaviour, through the imaginative sympathy of one individual for another's emotion.

The work of the French philosopher, Auguste Comte, whose *Positivist Philosophy* had been published in France in 1830, was popularized by G. H. Lewes and others in the 1850s and 1860s; his ideas drew together the analysis of human nature and the methodology and language of science and development, with an examination of societies. Comte saw societies as evolving through stages, from the 'Theological' to the 'Metaphysical' to the 'Positivist'. Different societies were at different stages in the process, which was one of progress. Just as societies evolve, he argued, human beings evolve (at varying rates according to their situations) from egoism to altruism. This evolution comes with maturation and education. In the proposal that human beings *progress* to altruism, Comte worked on the assumption that the individual exists most importantly as a member of a society. This social organism relied upon interaction and interdependence, an observation of social behaviour based on the scientific observation of the relations of all the elements of society. The new Positivist society would display a harmonious working together of the Intellect, Feeling, and Activity, terms that described for Comte an intellectual and scientific élite, women, and the working classes, respectively. Although this sounds divisive – and indeed, the implications for women and for the working classes were far-reaching, for Comte argued that they had fixed parts to play in a society which could only evolve gradually and according to fixed laws – it is evident that Feuerbach's emphasis on human feeling and sympathy coincides at certain points with Comte's vision of the role of the individual in society.

Comte contributed two ideas vital to George Eliot's outlook: the definition of historical processes as important, dynamic and progressive, and the vision of society as organic, where each part was necessary to the healthy action of the whole. The individual is located temporally and spatially in a network of roles and duties, and the importance of personal development is that it produces someone increasingly more socially benevolent. Positivism was to be a faith without God: a faith in social human beings. At the same time, Positivism reflected current trends in scientific thought, with its emphasis on temporal continuity and progress.

It appears that the later, more dogmatic Comte was less attractive in his ideas to thinkers such as George Eliot. Comte's conviction that the individual must submit to social duty leaves little scope for the individual. However, in exploring George Eliot's philosophy, the chain of logic seems to be as follows: human beings differ from animals in their faculties for emotion, affection and sympathy, which help to create a human *society* over and above the individual. At the same time, human beings are in chains to their physical and biological states. Morality can exist independently of a God if human beings are capable of altruism and of social duty. It is a supremely humanist vision, that the sympathy

19

with others can create – but certainly not merely coerce – a thoroughgoing moral, because social, behaviour. The ways in which these ideas are present in *Middlemarch* are manifold. Dorothea's story traces a development from initial blindness and egoism to an altruism that helps those around her. The society of Middlemarch is analysed as an interactive and organic community. Many egoists suffer and are forced to learn that the desires of others exert equal claims, and some acquire some sympathy and compassion for their fellows. All these issues will be discussed more fully in the later 'Commentary and Analysis'.

II *Contexts for* Middlemarch

1. History and the Novel

A novel's placing within time is always significant. Some novels are self-consciously up-to-date, some set in the future – and many in the past. *Middlemarch* is set in the years 1829 to 1832, but was written in the early 1870s. It carries the imprint of personal memory on George Eliot's part, but also marks the significance of a particular moment of historical change, for the first Reform Act was passed in 1832 and the second Reform Act in 1867.

History and time came to have a special, and new, importance for the Victorians. Differing versions of history were the topic of extended discussion in books and periodicals, and 'history', in its many forms, was widely read. Some professors of history – Arnold, Froude and Kingsley, for example – were also seen as public gurus, enjoying the close attention of the educated public. In general, the reading and interpretation of the past are closely tied in with the questions of what history is 'for', which or whose past it is appropriate to consider, and the relation of the past to the present. Thus, history might be studied for lessons, both exhortatory and precautionary, for the present. Depending on the historian's assessment of the present, history might demonstrate by contrast how the past was noble, moral and stable, or how the past was benighted, primitive and squalid. An attention to Roman history in the nineteenth century tended, for example, to foreground issues of rising British imperialism by comparison and contrast. It was in thinking about the present, to some extent, that Victorians turned to the past.

A great deal of the interest in history was romantic, deriving its inspiration from the novels of Sir Walter Scott, and although the study of history as a pursuit was not new it was given a seriousness and scrupulousness by German historians of the early nineteenth century. With the work of Barthold Niebuhr, whose *Roman History*, written in 1811–1812, was translated into English in 1828 and 1831, history began to attain the status of a discipline. Other German thinkers such as Leopold von Ranke and, later, Theodor Mommsen, eschewing the concept of history as a repository of moral lessons and anecdotes, or as an occasion for purely nationalistic self-congratulation, focused on the investigation of historical events. Ranke, who examined the archives of Vienna, Venice, Florence and Rome, and who stressed the importance of original sources, stated in a formulation that was to become famous:

History has had assigned to it the task of judging the past, of instructing the present for the benefit of ages to come. The present study does not assume such a high office; it wants to show only what happened.

The term 'natural history', so often used to describe the study of the natural world, and rising to such popularity in the nineteenth century, catches both the objective investigation characteristic of new ways of thinking, and the growing attention to the past. For evolutionary ideas also contributed to modern Victorian historiography: the concept of evolution presented a new way of perceiving time, as a developing continuum in which the past was intimately connected with the present and thereby had a determining effect on the future. Ways in which to interpret and describe the movement from past to present differed. The Whig school of history, which tended to predominate in the nineteenth century, concentrated on social and political trends, while Tory sympathizers found it possible to emphasize the emergence of great men, individuals who were capable of determining and directing events – hence Carlyle's glorification of heroes in *Heroes, Hero-Worship, and the Heroic in History* (1841).

When it was the pressure of the present times that drew the attention to the past, then questions about the nature of contemporary life and society became urgent. Signs of transition and change were evident everywhere during the nineteenth century in Britain. The proliferation of industrial and urban centres, with attendant pollution, overcrowding and inadequate social provision, could not be ignored. The rapid development of the railway system in the 1830s and 1840s changed the physical landscape and also enabled people to see far more easily and swiftly the circumstances in which others lived. As the historian Harold Perkin says,

The Industrial Revolution ... was more than an expansion of commerce, more than a series of changes in the technology of certain industries, more even than an acceleration of general economic growth. It was a revolution in men's access to the means of life ... Such a rise in the scale of life required, involved and implied drastic changes in society itself: in the size and distribution of the population, in its social structure and organization, and in the political and administrative superstructure which they demanded and supported. It was in brief *a social revolution*: a revolution in social organization, with social causes as well as social effects.[1]

Parliamentary reform took place, and enfranchisement was affected, albeit only partially. Subsequently legislation brought developments in education, social services, women's rights, and employment. What has been identified as the structure of the modern British economy emerged: not only was Britain in the mid nineteenth century the 'workshop' of the world, but the City of London was also its clearing-house. Banking, shipping, insurance: all became powerful and prominent.

Inevitably, responses to such overwhelming and perceptible changes were mixed. Outrage at distress, injustice and inequality echoes throughout the writings of Dickens, Mayhew and others. Yet in 1833 Macaulay wrote, 'The history of England is emphatically the history of progress', and he was by no means alone in his opinion. To produce these contending reactions, two things seem to have happened, partly to do with political developments in the early decades of the century. Firstly, a period of sweeping reform in the 1820s and 1830s led to a sense among the middle and upper classes that things had been achieved and that therefore gradual change rather than abrupt radicalism should now resume. Secondly, discontent at the lack of achievement through reform caused upheaval among the still disenfranchised working class, an upheaval that confirmed the middle-class distrust of reform and that led them to emphasize conservatism under the aegis of 'progress'. Hence, a distrust of the people, fuelled by not very distant memories of the French Revolution, collided with humanitarian concern about the evident inequities of British society. 'Progress' therefore came to signify the opposite of 'reform', and both terms assumed ideological and class-based connotations. In much Victorian writing there is a confused mixture of representations: the present as advanced and positive, with the past as primitive and squalid, vie for attention with representations of the present as squalid and intolerable set against some golden age in the past.

In part, it was the very speed of change that impressed Victorians. Many of the major Victorian writers who are still read today were born between 1810 and 1820: Gaskell, Thackeray, Browning, Dickens, Reade, Trollope, the Brontës, Eliot, Kingsley and Clough. Indeed, Queen Victoria herself was born in 1819. The perceptions of this generation were inevitably of the difference between the days of their childhood, before railways, reform and countless other innovations, and the days of their maturity: perceptions, then, that registered change and the speed of that change within the span of a lifetime. The railway, with its sudden arrival on the scene, and its unaccustomed speed of movement, provided an example of, and a metaphor for, increased tempo. In *Dombey and Son* (1848), Dickens describes Mr Dombey's journey from

London to Leamington Spa, after the untimely death of his young son:

Away, with a shriek, and a roar, and a rattle, plunging down into the earth again, and working on in such a storm of energy and perseverance, that amidst the darkness and whirlwind the motion seems reversed, and to tend furiously backward, until a ray of light upon the wet wall shows its surface flying past like a fierce stream. Away once more into the day, and through the day, with a shrill yell of exultation, roaring, rattling, tearing on, spurning everything with its dark breath, sometimes pausing for a minute where a crowd of faces are, that in a minute more are not; sometimes lapping water greedily, and before the spout at which it drinks has ceased to drip upon the ground, shrieking, roaring, rattling through the purple distance!

Louder and louder yet, it shrieks and cries as it comes tearing on resistless to the goal: and now its way, still like the way of Death, is strewn with ashes thickly. Everything around is blackened. There are dark pools of water, muddy lanes, and miserable habitations far below. There are jagged walls and falling houses close at hand, and through the battered roofs and broken windows, wretched rooms are seen, where want and fever hide themselves in many wretched shapes, while smoke and crowded gables, and distorted chimneys, and deformity of brick and mortar penning up deformity of mind and body, choke the murky distance ... it is never in his thoughts that the monster who has brought him there has let the light of day in on these things: not made or caused them.

Dickens captures here the jolting rhythm and sense of dislocation in early railway travel. To Mr Dombey the speed of the train becomes an image of the devouring energy of 'Death', personified. In the second paragraph quoted here, Dickens also conveys the pollution caused by steam combustion, the ashes reminiscent of death, and he moves on to contemplate the scenes which are revealed from the railway carriage window. His final comment firmly states that travellers like Mr Dombey cannot merely deplore what they see, for the railway reveals appalling social conditions; it does not create them.

George Eliot likewise achieves a striking series of similes in her reaction to innovations in transport, in *Felix Holt*, but her response is far more conservative:

Posterity may be shot, like a bullet through a tube, by atmospheric pressure from Winchester to Newcastle: that is a fine result to have among our hopes; but the slow old-fashioned way of getting from one end of our country to the other is the better thing to have in the memory. The tube-journey can never lend much to picture and narrative; it is as barren as an exclamatory O! Whereas the happy outside passenger seated on the box from the dawn to the gloaming gathered enough stories of English life, enough of English labours in towns and country, enough aspects of earth and sky, to make episodes for a modern Odyssey.

She proposes that a survey of England may more tellingly be made from a coach than from a railway carriage, and subsequently traces the gradual movement from settled rural scene to derelict hamlet and fractious town-life. The very speed of a future 'tube-journey' may, according to George Eliot, militate against the traveller's survey of social conditions.

Describing the difference between then and now, before and after, seen in this passage from *Felix Holt*, was a general habit among Victorian writers. Their experience of change was more sharply focused by being but a single 'moment' within the long perspective of time evoked by geological theories. In *In Memoriam* (1850), Tennyson speaks of the concept of prehistory:

> Contemplate all this work of Time
> . . . They say,
> The solid earth whereon we tread
>
> In tracts of fluent heat began,
>   And grew to seeming-random forms,
>   The seeming prey of cyclic storms,
> Till at the last arose the man . . .
>
> (CXVII)

Set within the long perspective of time, the changes of a mere forty or fifty years are emphasized, but also made terrifyingly insignificant.

By the turn of the nineteenth and twentieth centuries, this sense of the disturbing immediacy of change had been lost. For example, in Conan Doyle's stories, which began to appear in 1887 with the publication of *A Study in Scarlet*, the speed and reliability of the trains enable Sherlock Holmes to reach the scenes of his investigations within hours. In 'Silver Blaze', the railway provides the occasion for Holmes to act decisively, to be a thoroughly modern man in his swift consumption of the newspapers, and to display his powers of deduction:

'We have, I think, just time to catch our train at Paddington, and I will go further into the matter upon our journey. You would oblige me by bringing with you your excellent field-glass.'

And so it happened that an hour or so later I found myself in the corner of a first-class carriage, flying along, *en route* for Exeter, while Sherlock Holmes, with his sharp, eager face framed in his earflapped travelling cap, dipped rapidly into the bundle of fresh papers which he had procured at Paddington. We had left Reading far behind us before he thrust the last of them under the seat, and offered me his cigar-case.

27

'We are going well,' said he, looking out of the window and glancing at his watch. 'Our rate at present is fifty-three and a half miles an hour.'

'I have not observed the quarter-mile posts,' said I.

'Nor have I. But the telegraph posts upon this line are sixty yards apart, and the calculation is a simple one.'

Virginia Woolf, in 1925, gives her character Mrs Dalloway thoughts of future 'ruins of time, when London is a grass-grown path and all those hurrying along the pavements this Wednesday morning are but bones with a few wedding rings mixed up in their dust', but no annihilating gulf threatens at this intimation of time's perspectives. D. H. Lawrence's imagining of the humming-bird in 1923 is both awestruck and slightly comic in its playfulness:

> I can imagine, in some other world
> Primeval-dumb, far back
> In that most awful stillness, that only gasped and hummed,
> Humming-birds raced down the avenues.
>
> (Humming-Bird, ll. 1–4)

But for Victorians, the reactions were ones of fear and of a serious recognition of the historical present – their time, that is – as one that would pass, just as they had witnessed the passing of so much. They therefore also registered a self-consciousness about defining their times, their cultures, their national identity, for the future.

In Dickens's use of the railway in *Dombey and Son*, and in George Eliot's meditations on time in *Felix Holt*, two different responses are evident. The first is a way of revealing social conditions, of defining change as an increased knowledge; the second, a reflex of nostalgia at the conditions that have been lost. Almost all the major Victorian writers wrote at least one historical novel. George Eliot wrote three different kinds of historical novel before *Middlemarch*, and these demonstrate some of the various uses of the historical novel for the Victorians, and the way that different versions of 'history' were concurrently in existence. *The Mill on the Floss* (1860), for example, evokes childhood events and affections, the young Maggie Tulliver in many ways standing in for the young Mary Anne Evans seen through the eyes of the mature George Eliot. In *Romola* (1863), George Eliot turns her attention to fifteenth-century Florence, and this elicits from her a painstaking and scrupulous investigation of historical detail which she decided was necessary in order to represent this period. In *Felix Holt* (1866), on the other hand, she looks explicitly at a moment of political change in 1831. With the character of 'Felix Holt the Radical', the novel debates issues of reform, depicting workers drawn into a riot on polling day, and the Comtean alternative of gradual development through education, which is espoused by Felix.

In *Middlemarch*, these varying exercises in the historical imagination are subsumed to become more general reflections on time and change that are thematic. The novel is permeated with a historical understanding that may be described under three headings: firstly, the placing of events in a particular time, secondly, the methodology of history, and thirdly, an awareness of the concept of history itself.

It is possible to interpret the actual dating of *Middlemarch* in several ways. The eve of the 1832 Reform Act is a 'before' that is both a golden age of security and a benighted time of limitation. It may also be employed as a metaphor for a moment of change itself. This multi-faceted position can be seen in the varying reactions of critics. Raymond Williams says that *Middlemarch* is 'significantly a novel of a single community again; a small town just before the decisive historical changes', while Sumner Ferris takes the opposite view: 'characters are having to adjust themselves to a new world, not somehow to re-establish the old one for themselves ... *Middlemarch* seems to me ... to be actually investigating the changes (in social and political structure, for instance) that society did encounter in the decade before Victoria.'[2] There is a forty-year gap between the dating and the composition of the novel, and this allows George Eliot to reflect on a number of issues: on 'before' and 'after', on parallels between 1832 and 1867 (with the respective Reform Acts of those years standing as metaphors for repetition or similarity), on the relative merits of 'reform' and 'progress', and on the 1830s as one beginning for the society of the 1860s and 1870s.

It is relevant here to sketch in more fully the historical and political contexts of the novel's dating and composition. The 1832 Reform Act, in the words of E. J. Evans, a recent historian, 'deserves to be remembered as one of the most momentous pieces of legislation in the history of Britain'.[3] The years from 1827 to 1832 saw many changes and events: the Roman Catholic Emancipation Act of 1829, which enabled Roman Catholics to enter Parliament, and which produced a backlash of reaction; a succession of governments struggling with the issue of impending reform; a growing fear of the working class in the context of riots; the eventual passing of a third reform bill in June 1832 after the House of Lords had obstructed earlier bills (see *Middlemarch*, p. 871) and had been threatened with the creation of a sizeable number of pro-reform peers. 'Britain has never in modern times been closer to revolution than in the autumn of 1831', E. J. Evans continues, and 'reform was peacefully enacted in June 1832 not because noble lords were persuaded by the merits of the case, but because they feared the consequences of continued resistance'. Before 1832, the qualification to vote, and the places which returned members to Parliament, relied on custom and precedent dating back to the fifteenth century. Consequently by the early nineteenth century, not only were patronage and bribery common, but a great many constituencies were uncontested, and 'rotten boroughs' of under fifty votes still existed (each returning two members to Parliament), whilst the vast industrial centres went unrepresented. The 1832 Reform Act did not make the ballot secret, and therefore did not eradicate bribery or patronage. It actually reduced the electorate in some places, by stipulating for the first time a £10 property qualification in boroughs, which meant that the franchise was only really extended to small property owners of the middle class. However, a semblance of parliamentary democracy was achieved.

When George Eliot first noted her project of a novel called *Middlemarch* in her journal, at the beginning of 1869, the 1867 Reform Act was a matter of very recent memory. It had been designed to give the vote to the respectable working man, by extending the borough franchise to all householders. Although Gladstone introduced a reform bill in March 1866, his Liberal government was defeated. Demonstrations in his support, and in support of reform, and riots in Hyde Park, followed later that year. A Conservative government, led by Lord Derby, but effectively with Disraeli as its helmsman, carried through reform in the face of its inevitability in 1867, but to the accompaniment of middle-class misgivings, expressed almost hysterically, for example, in Carlyle's article, 'Shooting Niagara: and After?' of August 1867. After further riots, concerning Trade Unionism, Fenianism, and Roman Catholicism, in 1867, a Liberal government was returned by the reformed electorate in the general election of November 1868. Dover Wilson calls the years leading up to, and including, this Act, 'a temporary phase of intense political excitement'.[4] George Eliot's decision to write a novel set in the years preceding the 1832 Reform Act is far from accidental: after the furore surrounding the 1867 Reform Act it must have seemed to many observers that the schisms between the middle class and the working class, the social unrest, the pressure for reform, were all repetitions of a recent epoch.

Just as George Eliot greeted Darwin's *Origin of Species* with the comment, 'So the world gets on step by step towards brave clearness and honesty!', so *Middlemarch* expresses a sense of the virtues of change. But it is a Comtean idea of gradual improvement, disavowing abrupt alteration, that prevails. Dorothea begins her story as an ardent would-be reformer, and ends it by distantly contributing to progress through her marriage to a radical Member of Parliament. The novel concludes with the reminder that

the growing good of the world is partly dependent on unhistoric acts; and that things are not so ill with you and me as they might have been, is half owing to the number who lived faithfully a hidden life, and rest in unvisited tombs. (p. 896)

'Hidden lives' can contribute to the progress of history; Dorothea's way is wholly endorsed in these words. Yet change *is* necessary, for Dorothea has also, in another sense, been wasted: living when she did, there was little opportunity for her to exercise her gifts more fully or effectively. As George Eliot says, earlier in the Finale, 'no one stated exactly what else that was in her power she ought rather to have done' (p. 894) – but paradoxically, *her* way, in the 1830s, has led to increasing 'goodness' in the 1870s. The reader, then, is meant simultaneously to admire Dorothea's contribution to the onward march of progress, and to pity her for finding herself in a relatively unwelcoming epoch.

This leads on to a consideration of the way in which the 'before' of the years of the novel, leading up to 1832, is regarded in the novel. There is much affectionate detailing of provincial life in an era before many changes, but there is also a constant awareness of the lack of opportunity, the lack of travel, the lack of communication, an awareness only achieved with the benefit of hindsight. Middlemarch itself, as a provincial town, is limited and limiting: we see this in Lydgate's experiences, Rosamond's (albeit snobbish) yearnings to escape, in the ridicule directed at Dorothea, and in her limited horizons that become painfully obvious when she encounters the culture and history of Rome. We see its pressure towards conformity, too, in the power and prevalence of gossip, public opinion and rumour, which travel fast and have considerable influence on the fates of the characters. However, this geographical constriction is not only to do with *provincial* life, which will be discussed more fully later, but it is also a function of the historical times within which the town exists. Middlemarch in the years 1829 to 1832 is a town without railways, an advanced postal system, or a modern network of newspapers. It is subject to the limited parliamentary representation of pre-reform days. It is small enough for many people to know each other and to be related to one another.

Yet despite the observations of limitations, George Eliot does not deplore Middlemarch. Several authorial asides remind the reader that condescending notions of the 'old-fashioned' or the 'defunct' are inaccurate. For example, we are told that, in contemplating Dorothea, 'All people, young or old (that is, all people in those ante-reform times), would have thought her an interesting object' (p. 50). This humorously draws a distinction between people before and after reform, a distinction which, it is implied, does not exist – therefore, the passage warns the reader not to dismiss Dorothea. The author mocks the reader's sense of supposed superiority to the past in another, similar parenthesis: 'her straw-bonnet (which our contemporaries might look at with conjectural curiosity as at an obsolete form of basket) fell a little backward' (p. 49). Fashions in dress, here, are simplistic indices of the difference between past and present.

There is, however, more ambiguity when the author considers education. In the following passage, the author returns to the changes of fashion in clothes, but raises the question of how far knowledge has accumulated between the past and the present. To Lydgate, at ten years old,

knowledge seemed to him a very superficial affair, easily mastered: judging from the conversation of his elders, he had apparently got already more than was necessary for mature life. Probably this was not an exceptional result of expensive teaching at that period of short-waisted coats, and other fashions which have not yet recurred. (p. 172)

Dorothea's 'slight regard for domestic music and feminine fine art must be forgiven her, considering the small tinkling and smearing in which they chiefly consisted at that dark period' (p. 89). With the case of the medical profession, the tone is yet more sombre:

it must be remembered that this was a dark period; and in spite of venerable colleges which used great efforts to secure purity of knowledge by making it scarce, and to exclude error by a rigid exclusiveness in relation to fees and appointments, it happened that very ignorant young gentlemen were promoted in town, and many more got a legal right to practise over large areas in the country. (pp. 174–5)

Yet even in this instance, the 'dark period' provides reformers and other young people in the novel with opportunities for optimism, for looking towards a different future. Indeed, there appear to be two perspectives existing concurrently: the optimism of youth, which we see in Lydgate, Dorothea and Ladislaw, all on the threshold of their adult lives, and the author's position of privileged retrospection, from which she discerns the existence of an inherent optimism in the years 1829 to 1832. Discussing Lydgate, George Eliot says, 'Perhaps that was a more cheerful time for observers and theorizers than the present' (p. 176). Likewise, apropos of Ladislaw, the Finale comments on 'those times when reforms were begun with a young hopefulness of immediate good which has been much checked in our days' (p. 894).

Book II of *Middlemarch* is entitled 'Old and Young', and focuses on the conflicts experienced by young men, Fred Vincy, Ladislaw, Lydgate, with old men, Featherstone, Casaubon, and even, perhaps, Bulstrode. They are conflicts which reflect the social and intellectual change of the period, change expressed, for example, by Featherstone when he says to Fred, '"God A'mighty sticks to the land. He promises land, and He gives land, and He makes chaps rich with corn and cattle. But you take the other side. You like Bulstrode and speckilation better than Featherstone and land"' (p. 138). Fred Vincy has to develop a new kind of career after his disappointment over Featherstone's will, but rejects the traditional university pathway of becoming a clergyman which, to his father, represents upward social mobility. By the time of the Finale, he has become 'a theoretic and practical farmer' (p. 890). The delicate nuances of changing social class, the incursion of new ways of earning a living, developments in savings, investments and trade, are all touched upon by George Eliot in Chapter 11:

Some slipped a little downward, some got higher footing: people denied aspirates, gained wealth, and fastidious gentlemen stood for boroughs; some were caught in political currents, some in ecclesiastical, and perhaps found themselves surprisingly grouped in consequence; while a few personages or families that stood with rock firmness amid all this fluctuation, were slowly presenting new aspects in spite of solidity, and altering with the double change of self and beholder. Municipal town and rural parish gradually made fresh threads of connection – gradually, as the old stocking gave way to the savings-bank, and the worship of the solar guinea became extinct, while squires and baronets, and even lords who had once lived blamelessly afar from the civic mind, gathered the faultiness of close acquaintanceship. Settlers, too, came from distant counties, some with an alarming novelty of skill, others with an offensive advantage in cunning. (p. 122)

Another young man is Ladislaw, who, like Lydgate and the young Bulstrode years before, has to encounter distrust because he is an outsider, one of these new 'settlers', and who, like Fred, must find a new kind of career. However, not only does Ladislaw find it difficult to be accepted, but he also has to contend with Casaubon's directive patronage and jealousy of a younger man. The painful resistance of the old world to the advent of the new is seen in the attitudes of both Featherstone and Casaubon – and in their later paralleling as 'dead hands', wishing to determine events after their deaths. (This is signalled by the title of Book V.)

33

A more extended parallel is drawn between Casaubon and Lydgate. Here, there is no 'conflict', Lydgate attending Casaubon respectfully in his last illness. There is even some thematic similarity between them, in that they are both searching for a 'key' in their respective studies: Casaubon seeks the 'Key to All Mythologies', while Lydgate wants to find 'some common basis' to the tissues of the human body (p. 177). But one is 'old', while the other is 'young': Casaubon

took a wife, as we have seen, to adorn the remaining quadrant of his course, and be a little moon that would cause hardly a calculable perturbation. But Lydgate was young, poor, ambitious. He had his half-century before him instead of behind him, and he had come to Middlemarch bent on doing many things that were not directly fitted to make his fortune or even secure him a good income. To a man under such circumstances, taking a wife is something more than a question of adornment . . . (p. 121)

Casaubon, described by Sir James rather passionately as '"no better than a mummy"' (p. 81), represents the death of an old, unproductive world of gentlemanly scholarship; Lydgate adumbrates future developments, future practices: 'He was at a starting-point which makes many a man's career a fine subject for betting' (p. 178). Casaubon looks back to history, while Lydgate looks forward to new discoveries; in their contrast lies a vista of change. This is also 'patterned' in the novel by their roles as bridegrooms, the one too old, the other unprepared.

When Virginia Woolf called *Middlemarch* 'one of the few English novels written for grown-up people',[5] it may be that she was partly indicating the shift from youthful optimism to middle-aged compromise, a shift, perhaps, most telling to readers who have themselves grown into some degree of disillusion. Dorothea's complex position in the novel with regard to reform, optimism, disillusion and progress has already been touched upon. Lydgate's experiences are the occasion of a fuller analysis. The 'growth of an intellectual passion' described in Chapter 15 shows both vocation and choice of profession. Lydgate resembles Dorothea in his spiritual and emotional dedication, and he also resembles Fred Vincy and Ladislaw in his development of a new means of employment, specific to the historical moment. Like Dorothea, again, he is a would-be reformer, having been attracted to medicine partly because it 'wanted reform' (p. 174). The link between political reform and medicine which is symbolically present in *Middlemarch* was made by George Eliot in a memorandum where she cited as major changes, 'the first Reform Bill' and 'the better understanding of disease'. Lydgate wishes to reform medicine both in its professional practice and in its scientific procedures. He has been educated at the three top centres for medicine of that period – London, Edinburgh and Paris – and thereby possesses unusually high and relevant qualifications. He is extremely up-to-date in his determination 'to act stoutly on the strength of a recent legal decision, and simply prescribe, without dispensing drugs or taking percentage from druggists' (p. 176). His treatment of Fred Vincy's fever is directed by his reading of Pierre-Charles Louis's 'new book on fever' (p. 193), published in the late 1820s, which he reads in Chapter 16. With Casaubon, he 'used his stethoscope (which had not become a matter of course in practice at that time)' (p. 320). His preferred treatment of Raffles follows Dr John Ware's *Remarks on the History and Treatment of Delirium Tremens*, published in 1831:

Lydgate rode away, forming no conjectures, in the first instance, about the history of Raffles, but rehearsing the whole argument which had lately been much stirred by the publication of Dr Ware's abundant experience in America, as to the right way of treating cases of alcoholic poisoning such as this. (p. 753)

Lydgate represents the future of his profession, and the new professionalization of medicine, and many of his experiences as a general practitioner in Middlemarch symbolize provincial resistance to the inevitable, progressive 'new', seen from the author's perspective of the 1870s. In his research, Lydgate is also up-to-date; in fact, he is really before his time: 'Does it seem incongruous to you that a Middlemarch surgeon should dream of himself as a discoverer? ... about 1829 the dark territories of Pathology were a fine America for a spirited young adventurer' (pp. 175, 177). His modernity is placed by his desire to extend the insights of Bichat, and by the fact that his tutor in Paris was Broussais. When he tells Farebrother, '"Raspail and others are on the same track, and I have been losing time"' (p. 495), this reference may be glossed with the information that Raspail announced his success in 1833.

Despite being a representative, in the novel, of youth, optimism and the future, as an individual character Lydgate is frustrated and fails. His 'spots of commonness', his refusal to recognize early enough the pressures of provincial society, his slightly misdirected research, are all given as reasons for his personal failure. Yet he also, in a rather contradictory way, is made to demonstrate an inevitable growth into middle age:

in the multitude of middle-aged men who go about their vocations in a daily course determined for them much in the same way as the tie of their cravats, there is always a good number who once meant to shape their own deeds and alter the world a little. The story of their coming to be shapen after the average and fit to be packed by the gross, is hardly ever told even in their consciousness; for perhaps their ardour in generous unpaid toil cooled as imperceptibly as the ardour of other youthful loves, till one day their earlier self walked like a ghost in its old home and made the new furniture ghastly. Nothing in the world more subtle than the process of their gradual change! (pp. 173–4)

George Eliot's complex and profound study of Lydgate raises many issues, some apparently contradictory. *Middlemarch*, in rejecting schematic themes or characterization, depicts individuals in more than one, or even several, guises. Thus Casaubon, as we have seen, represents the 'old', the demise of a former world, but his presence in the novel, and the nature of his research, reminds the reader of the 1870s of another future, one that is mischievously referred to by Ladislaw in Rome:

'it is a pity that it should be thrown away, as so much English scholarship is, for want of knowing what is being done by the rest of the world. If Mr Casaubon read German he would save himself a great deal of trouble.' (p. 240)

The late 1820s and the 1830s of *Middlemarch* have the additional significance of being the early years of the incursion of German scholarship and methodology, which were to have such a marked effect on British philosophy and religion. Some of the texts already mentioned here date from this period: Niebuhr's *Roman History* in its English translation (1828 and 1831), Strauss's *Das Leben Jesu* (1835), and even Feuerbach's *Wesen das Christentums* (1841). Indeed, Ladislaw's taunt amounts to a semi-private reference by George Eliot to her own influence on British thought through her translations of Strauss and Feuerbach. Casaubon's ignorance of German thought, then, contributes to a general theme in the novel of the growth of knowledge. Here, the dates of other publications should also be noted: Comte's *Positivist Philosophy* of 1830, Lyell's *Principles of Geology* (1830–1833), and Hennell's *Inquiry into the Origins of Christianity* (1838).

Not only are the intellectual problems of the nineteenth century treated in *Middlemarch*, but political events, and especially the very significant Reform Act, are carefully woven into the story. The novel begins with Casaubon's courtship of Dorothea, and with Lydgate's arrival in Middlemarch. This is dated, in Chapter 15, as being during the autumn of 1829. It draws to a close with the news of Dorothea's engagement to Ladislaw, in the spring of 1832, pinpointed by a reference at the beginning of Chapter 84: 'It was just after the Lords had thrown out the Reform Bill' (p. 871), which occurred in May 1832. The novel ends its action just before the marriage of Dorothea and Ladislaw, and also just before the passing of the Reform Act on 7 June 1832. In the course of the novel, characters discuss wider political events; most prominently, it is Mr Brooke who refers to them, and who participates in them, with his candidature during the general election of May 1831. Yet in this instance, a major national event is overshadowed by the immediate effects of Casaubon's death and will. 'History' as a catalogue of month-by-month events in the arena of national politics coexists with the lives (and deaths) of individuals. This national history is shown to have profound effects on individuals and communities, but it also occurs for most of the time 'off-stage': day-to-day life figures more highly in human beings' minds.

Middlemarch refers to the events leading up to June 1832 in order to present these more general issues of history, which are often prompted by a particular historical moment. And in considering history, the novel confronts time. It is carefully plotted to trace the months between autumn 1829 and spring 1832, but it also conflates a dynamic of change with a picture of simultaneity. Changes are occurring at different stages and at different rates within a very short space of time. The novel appears at once to emphasize movement and to focus on a particular period. We may observe that it is an uncharacteristic novel of its era in its limitation to such a very short span of time: there is no exploration of either a backward or a forward vista.

The contrasts between the 'histories' of individuals' lives and the 'history' of events in politics or medicine or scholarship are evident throughout *Middlemarch*, and lead to more philosophical considerations of the concept of history and the nature of time. George Eliot frequently draws the reader's attention to history, as when she calls Rome 'the city of visible history, where the past of a whole hemisphere seems moving in funeral procession with strange ancestral images and trophies gathered from afar' (p. 224). The Prelude begins with a sentence that refers to both history and time: 'Who that cares much to know the history of man, and how the mysterious mixture behaves under the varying experiments of Time ...' (p. 25) Famous historians, such as Josephus and Herodotus, are mentioned by name. In addition, in an emphatic paragraph at the beginning of Chapter 15, George Eliot relates the writing of history to the writing of fiction. She compares her task with that of Henry Fielding, and refers to him as 'A great historian' (p. 170). Yet she differentiates between his self-appointed role and her own:

Fielding lived when the days were longer (for time, like money, is measured by our needs), when summer afternoons were spacious, and the clock ticked slowly in the winter evenings. We belated historians must not linger after his example; and if we did so, it is probable that our chat would be thin and eager, as if delivered from a camp-stool in a parrot-house. I at least have so much to do in unravelling certain human lots, and seeing how they were woven and interwoven, that all the light I can command must be concentrated on this particular web, and not dispersed over that tempting range of relevancies called the universe. (p. 170)

Time, according to this passage, has 'speeded up', and history becomes focused increasingly on 'certain human lots', thereby questioning the 'range of relevancies called the universe', however tempting they may be. It is a famous passage, in which George Eliot renounces the ambitions of time and space in order to concentrate on a small sample, a 'particular web'. Within this web, however, she suggests, there lies the implication of all historical change and development. The people of Middlemarch, in their interaction and experience, can be seen as embodying history.

2. Causation and Coincidence

I remember how, at Cambridge, I walked with her once in the Fellows' Garden of Trinity, on an evening of rainy May: and she, stirred somewhat beyond her wont, and taking as her text the three words which have been used so often as the inspiring trumpet-calls of men, – the words *God, Immortality, Duty,* – pronounced, with terrible earnestness, how inconceivable was the *first,* how unbelievable the *second,* and yet how peremptory and absolute the *third.* Never, perhaps, have sterner accents affirmed the sovereignty of impersonal and un-recompensing Law. I listened, and night fell; her grave, majestic countenance turned towards me like a sibyl's in the gloom; it was as though she withdrew from my grasp, one by one, the two scrolls of promise, and left me the third scroll only, awful with inevitable fates. And when we stood at length and parted, amid that columnar circuit of the forest-trees, beneath the last twilight of star-less skies, I seemed to be gazing, like Titus at Jerusalem, on vacant seats and empty halls, – on a sanctuary with no Presence to hallow it, and heaven left lonely of a God.

F. W. H. Myers composed this memory of George Eliot in the year following her death.[6] It is, like George Eliot herself on the evening in question, terribly earnest in evoking how the Fellows' Garden of Trinity College, Cambridge, was transformed for her listener into a friendless and post-apocalyptic universe. The conversation was moment-ous, and Myers's description expresses many features familiar to readers of George Eliot's fiction. In finding God and immortality incredible, she turns to the substitute of duty, which has 'the sovereignty of impersonal and unrecompensing Law'. This famous memory makes explicit the logical connections between three ideas: God is replaced by duty and by a sense of causality derived largely from scientific and evolutionary thinking. Biological and physiological imperatives unite with obeisance to a social ideal: 'how peremptory and absolute' was *Duty*.

From the earliest days of her writing career, George Eliot held the opinion that there are no exceptions to the order of nature. Reviewing Robert Mackay's *The Progress of the Intellect* in 1851, she talks of 'undeviating law', 'invariability of sequence', and 'that inexorable law of consequences'. These phrases show that the 'law' of which she speaks is an evolutionary law of movement and development through time, and that it is a law that will not be diverted or halted. Writing in 1865, in a review of William Lecky's work, entitled 'The Influence of

Rationalism', she refers to 'the great conception of universal regular sequence, without partiality and without caprice'. Scientific observation earns her approbation in both reviews, and she sees 'law' as imposing a version of ethical behaviour. It is important to note here, that to George Eliot, and to others who shared her point of view, there was no inherent contradiction between the progress of ethics and the evolution of species. Indeed, these issues were easily reconciled; it was only in the minds of opponents that a painful contradiction was experienced between the claims of science and the ethics of human behaviour. In 1851, George Eliot wrote,

The divine yea and nay, the seal of prohibition and of sanction, are effectually impressed on human deeds and aspirations, not by means of Greek and Hebrew, but by that inexorable law of consequences, whose evidence is confirmed instead of weakened as the ages advance; and human duty is comprised in the earnest study of this law and patient obedience to its teaching.

However, the impersonality of such a law struck many Victorians as unregarding of the individual life. As Tennyson says, in *In Memoriam*, 'So careful of the type she seems,/ So careless of the single life'. George Eliot recognizes the burden of natural law, and transforms it into a basis for ethics. But such a view tends to lead to a deterministic interpretation of events and experience, and throughout her work, there is debate about the extent of free will and determinism, and a sense of the tragedy of the impersonal forces that impinge upon the individual.

In *Middlemarch*, it is pre-eminently the plotting that demonstrates George Eliot's notions of law. Just as evolution takes place slowly and inexorably, so trains of events, actions and choices gradually build up in the course of the novel. These produce outcomes often ironic in reversal and often disappointing to the individual character. 'What happens', then, is not dramatic or sudden, but slow and almost imperceptible to the character. There is a minor instance of this in the authorial comment discussing Mr Vincy's failure to prevent the marriage of Rosamond and Lydgate: 'in the meanwhile the hours were each leaving their little deposit and gradually forming the final reason for inaction, namely, that action was too late' (p. 380). Here, time itself forms a kind of geological deposit, hardening his inaction, until it becomes, paradoxically, a decision not to act.

A couple of specific examples of plotting may be traced quite easily. In Chapter 29, letters arrive for both Dorothea and Casaubon from

Ladislaw, and Casaubon's immediate refusal to entertain Ladislaw irritates Dorothea and leads to a disagreement between the couple. In Dorothea, 'Pity, that "newborn babe" which was by-and-by to rule many a storm within her, did not "stride the blast" on this occasion' (p. 316). Half an hour later, Casaubon suffers his first heart attack: this is the first step in his dying, and in Dorothea's growth towards sympathetic pity. During Casaubon's recovery, Dorothea reads Ladislaw's letters and realizes that his intended arrival must be swiftly averted, so she asks her uncle to reply on her behalf. Mr Brooke's letter lurches erratically from point to point, just as greater chains of events do:

It expressed regrets and proposed remedies, which, when Mr Brooke read them, seemed felicitously worded – surprisingly the right thing, and determined a sequel which he had never before thought of. In this case, his pen found it such a pity that young Ladislaw should not have come into the neighbourhood just at that time, in order that Mr Brooke might make his acquaintance more fully, and that they might go over the long-neglected Italian drawings together – it also felt such an interest in a young man who was starting in life with a stock of ideas – that by the end of the second page it had persuaded Mr Brooke to invite young Ladislaw, since he could not be received at Lowick, to come to Tipton Grange. (pp. 325–6)

It is while a large gathering watches Featherstone's funeral from an upstairs window at Lowick that Celia recognizes Ladislaw, and Brooke explains that Ladislaw is his guest. The misunderstanding deepens between Casaubon and Dorothea, partly because she cannot explain to him in front of the others, and ironically, Ladislaw is established in Middlemarch in precisely the way that Casaubon would not have wished. His appearance begins the promptings that are to cause Casaubon to rewrite his will:

His antipathy to Will did not spring from the common jealousy of a winter-worn husband: it was something deeper, bred by his lifelong claims and discontents; but Dorothea, now that she was present – Dorothea, as a young wife who herself had shown an offensive capability of criticism, necessarily gave concentration to the uneasiness which had before been vague. (p. 395)

Another example concerns Brooke's decision to stand as an Independent candidate, in favour of Reform. In Chapter 39, Dorothea visits him to exhort him to improve his estate, partly because Sir James feels that Brooke will be pilloried for bad management. Like so many of Dorothea's endeavours, this fails – but it succeeds in an ironic way after she has left him at Dagley's farm, for there he is roundly abused: 'He walked out of the yard as quickly as he could, in some amazement at the novelty of his situation. He had never been insulted on his own land before, and had been inclined to regard himself as a general favourite' (p. 432). In the following chapter, Caleb Garth receives a letter from Sir James inviting him to act as agent for his estate of Freshitt and also for Brooke's estate of Tipton. The opportunity means that Mary will not have to go away to teach, as the family will have more money, and in the course of the same chapter comes news of Fred's decisions to retake his degree and not to become a clergyman. By the end of the chapter, Garth has decided to offer Fred a job at some time in the future: '"I shall want help, and Fred might come in and learn the nature of things and act under me, and it might be the making of him into a useful man, if he gives up being a parson"' (p. 445). Thus, in a seemingly haphazard series of events, the futures of both Mary and Fred are assured because of Brooke's political ambitions. This particular example is highlighted by the author at the beginning of Chapter 40:

In watching effects, if only of an electric battery, it is often necessary to change our place and examine a particular mixture or group at some distance from the point where the movement we are interested in was set up. The group I am moving towards is at Caleb Garth's breakfast-table . . . (p. 434)

George Eliot seems to be remarking on the nature of plotting when she includes a comic interlude in Chapter 57. Mrs Garth has been led on by her irritation with Fred to tell him that Farebrother is also fond of Mary; she then regrets it, and wishes to check the 'unintended consequences' of the conversation (p. 620). Then,

while she was hesitating there was already a rush of unintended consequences under the apple-tree where the tea-things stood. Ben, bouncing across the grass with Brownie at his heels, and seeing the kitten dragging the knitting by a lengthening line of wool, shouted and clapped his hands; Brownie barked, the kitten, desperate, jumped on the tea-table and upset the milk, then jumped down again and swept half the cherries with it; and Ben, snatching up the half-knitted sock-top, fitted it over the kitten's head as a new source of madness, while Letty arriving cried out to her mother against this cruelty – it was a history as full of sensation as 'This is the house that Jack built.' (pp. 620–1)

Middlemarch is not 'a history . . . full of sensation' like this domestic upset, for events do not occur so swiftly or so physically on the whole. However, in the way that each incident springs from a cause and produces an effect, and in the accidental quality of the plotting, the novel does resemble this small chain of events.

Evolutionary law stresses not only the passage of time, but also the active role played by the environment in 'what happens'. Transferred to a philosophical debate about human life, the environment becomes 'conditions', or the social network, within which each individual exists. Therefore, not only may the individual partly be able to determine future events by his or her actions, but his or her social environment also plays a decisive part. Irony arises from the unavoidable accretion of circumstances through time, and also through the impersonal workings of conditions. In this world without God, there is no divine plan: it is a bleak prospect that produces irony and disillusionment, and indeed, many readers find *Middlemarch* sad, pessimistic, or even tragic. Lydgate's troubles, for example, are compounded by the social milieu in which he finds himself.

The 'rush of unintended consequences' lightly shown at Mrs Garth's tea-table is joined by 'the irony of events' and 'the force of circumstances', all general phrases employed by George Eliot in the course of the novel. In Chapter 46, for example, it is the irony of national politics and events that throws Farebrother and Bulstrode into the same camp, in favour of reform. In Chapter 36,

Mr Vincy, blustering as he was, had as little of his own way as if he had been a prime minister: the force of circumstances was easily too much for him, as it is for most pleasure-loving florid men; and the circumstance called Rosamond was particularly forcible by means of that mild persistence which, as we know, enables a white soft living substance to make its way in spite of opposing rock. (p. 379)

A similar version of experience, according to George Eliot, occurs within the individual: she comments that 'character too is a process and an unfolding' (p. 178). Thus Lydgate's reactions and actions reflect and mould the maturing man, while a series of events – his courtship of and marriage to Rosamond, his professional career, his mounting debts – unrolls in dynamic interrelation with his character. In a much later conversation, Lydgate is once again the topic: Dorothea wishes to defend him against the accusations that are rife:

'there is a man's character beforehand to speak for him.'
    'But, my dear Mrs Casaubon,' said Mr Farebrother, smiling gently at her ardour, 'character is not cut in marble – it is not something solid and unalterable. It is something living and changing, and may become diseased as our bodies do.'
    'Then it may be rescued and healed,' said Dorothea. (pp. 790–1)

Time's span of past, present and future, brought to the fore by scientific insights, is implicit in the emphasis on how past actions and events have their inevitable effects in the present and will be discernible in future consequences. Once again, there is considerable irony disclosed by the examples in the novel. Lydgate thinks that he can see into the future of his marriage: 'having been accepted, he was prepared to accept all the consequences which he believed himself to foresee with perfect clearness' (p. 382). Immediately following this sentence there comes a description of his expensive tastes in setting up home. Ladislaw, too, meditates on consequences when he finds that his journalism has set a social distance between him and Dorothea:

his irritation had gone out towards Mr Casaubon, who had declared beforehand that Will would lose caste. 'I never had any caste,' he would have said, if that prophecy had been uttered to him, and the quick blood would have come and gone like breath in his transparent skin. But it is one thing to like defiance, and another thing to like its consequences. (p. 502)

The awareness of the continuum of time also appears in *Middlemarch* in a certain reverence for the past. So, for some characters, and for some plots within the novel, the past becomes a benevolent sanctity determining a happy future. This is particularly evident in the Fred Vincy/Mary Garth plot. Mary tells Farebrother:

'I have too strong a feeling for Fred to give him up for any one else. I should never be quite happy if I thought he was unhappy for the loss of me. It has taken such deep root in me – my gratitude to him for always loving me best, and minding so much if I hurt myself, from the time when we were very little. I cannot imagine any new feeling coming to make that weaker.' (p. 561)

She foregoes the future possibility of a marriage to Farebrother, preferring to nurture her long-standing affection for Fred. Yet although that particular happiness comes to fruition, there is always the threat of change in the passage of time, and through the process and unfolding of character. Farebrother warns Fred later, '"relations of this sort, even when they are of long standing, are always liable to change"' (p. 727).

In *Middlemarch*, George Eliot does not merely provide the reader with plot, but examines the process of plot itself, posing the question: what makes what happens happen? This is a profound question, implicating religion and science. She also turns her attention to equally profound questions of the basis of action and interaction – do human beings act with a sense of security in a divine plan, or with a pessimistic sense of determinism, or do they take responsibility for themselves and

and their actions? The very notion of change, present when Farebrother warns Fred, and more generally present in an evolutionary view of life, has the power to signify differing things: it reflects a pessimism that there is an inexorable law of motion and development, yet it also holds out the possibility that human beings can learn and progress.

And it is possible to suggest that, in *Middlemarch*, the story of Lydgate demonstrates the workings of law through character, actions and environment, while the story of Dorothea demonstrates the escape from such a deterministic version of experience. George Eliot proffers a solution to the bleak prospect of a world without God that her plotting reveals. It is a solution that calls on the philosophies of Feuerbach and Spinoza, discussed earlier: the individual's suffering creates a sympathy with others and a desire not to harm others. In an article on the poet Young, published in 1857, George Eliot contrasts one kind of religious view with her own philosophy most clearly. Young, in her opinion, implies that only the prospect of an after-life can rule moral behaviour:

We can imagine the man who 'denies his soul immortal', replying, 'It is quite possible that *you* would be a knave, and love yourself alone, if it were not for your belief in immortality; but you are not to force upon me what would result from your own utter want of moral emotion. I am just and honest, not because I expect to live in another world, but because, having felt the pain of injustice and dishonesty towards myself, I have a fellow-feeling with other men, who would suffer the same pain if I were unjust or dishonest towards them.'

In *Middlemarch*, there is a covert reference to George Eliot's disagreement with Young when Mr Brooke refers to a Methodist preacher arrested for poaching:

'I thought Flavell looked very little like "the highest style of man" – as somebody calls the Christian – Young, the poet Young, I think – you know Young? Well, now, Flavell in his shabby black gaiters, pleading that he thought the Lord had sent him and his wife a good dinner, and he had a right to knock it down, though not a mighty hunter before the Lord, as Nimrod was – I assure you it was rather comic.' (p. 428)

This mocking reference to hypocrisy and reliance on Providence in a religious man foreshadows Bulstrode, of course.

Dorothea's character unfolds as she undergoes a series of lessons in *Middlemarch*: she learns from these lessons, she changes and achieves some release from powerlessness and ironic disappointment. And what she learns, in this context, is loss of egoism, and the acquisition of sympathy and altruism. From the early choice of a martyrdom that she is too young and too short-sighted to recognize, she develops sympathy with others through her marriage to Casaubon:

she had felt the waking of a presentiment that there might be a sad consciousness in his life which made as great a need on his side as on her own.

We are all of us born in moral stupidity, taking the world as an udder to feed our supreme selves: Dorothea had early begun to emerge from that stupidity, but yet it had been easier to her to imagine how she would devote herself to Mr Casaubon, and become wise and strong in his strength and wisdom, than to conceive with that distinctness which is no longer reflection but feeling – an idea wrought back to the directness of sense, like the solidity of objects – that he had an equivalent centre of self, whence the lights and shadows must always fall with a certain difference. (p. 243)

We follow Dorothea through the meticulous detailing of her life with Casaubon, and through the effects on her of her widowhood and his will. The culmination of her change is reached when she is capable of understanding the potentially tragic situation for Lydgate, Rosamond and Ladislaw, after she has witnessed, as she thinks, a compromising scene between Rosamond and Ladislaw. She quells her own jealousy and distress, and resolves to act to help matters:

All the active thought with which she had before been representing to herself the trials of Lydgate's lot, and this young marriage union which, like her own, seemed to have its hidden as well as evident troubles – all this vivid sympathetic experience returned to her now as a power: it asserted itself as acquired knowledge asserts itself and will not let us see as we saw in the day of our ignorance. She said to her own irremediable grief, that it should make her more helpful, instead of driving her back from effort.

And what sort of crisis might not this be in three lives whose contact with hers laid an obligation on her as if they had been suppliants bearing the sacred branch? ... 'What should I do – how should I act now, this very day if I could clutch my own pain, and compel it to silence, and think of those three!' (p. 846)

To Dorothea, contact with others creates in her an obligation towards them: this is the duty of being a social individual. It is the duty which follows 'law' but which transforms it into a basis for ethics.

The imagery of the novel conveys this aspect of *Middlemarch* carefully and extensively. The 'particular web' is an image both of constriction and of human interdependence. The threads of the web are both chains and channels for human effort towards others, seen poignantly, for example, in the description of Rosamond's and Lydgate's newly declared love:

Young love-making – that gossamer web! Even the points it clings to – the things whence its subtle interlacings are swung – are scarcely perceptible; momentary touches of finger-tips, meetings of rays from blue and dark orbs, unfinished phrases, lightest changes of cheek and lip, faintest tremors. The web itself is made of spontaneous beliefs and indefinable joys, yearnings of one life towards another, visions of completeness, indefinite trust. (p. 380)

Initially, this web is symbolic of the impulses towards another human being; in the case of Rosamond and Lydgate it is to become a prison of misunderstanding and failure. In another set of images, Dorothea finds herself in the darkness of a labyrinth, and of a tomb, hemmed in by social constraints and by Casaubon's limited world: 'To-day she had stood at the door of the tomb and seen Will Ladislaw receding into the distant world of warm activity and fellowship – turning his face towards her as he went' (p. 516). Eventually she is to reach the light and warmth of freedom with him. The imagery of the novel will be discussed more fully later.

Those characters who do not recognize duty, or who even wilfully refuse to admit the existence of duty, like to pretend that they exist within a theistic universe. Their egoism generally allows them to believe that events are arranged for their desire or convenience, and that 'Providence' is working on their behalf. Casaubon, so centred on himself and on his work, tends to feel that Dorothea was created for his benefit: 'Providence, in its kindness, had supplied him with the wife he needed . . . Whether Providence had taken equal care of Miss Brooke in presenting her with Mr Casaubon was an idea which could hardly occur to him' (p. 313). Mr Vincy genially believes in Providence, and this belief reflects his inherent optimism:

'I think I was justified in what I tried to do for Fred. If you come to religion, it seems to me a man shouldn't want to carve out his meat to an ounce beforehand: – one must trust a little to Providence and be generous.' (p. 156)

In fact, this seems to be a family trait, for Mrs Vincy later says, '"I feel as sure as I sit here, Fred will turn out well – else why was he brought back from the brink of the grave?"' (p. 377), and Fred is rather comically described in his disappointment over the amount of Featherstone's early cash gift: 'What can the fitness of things mean, if not their fitness to a man's expectations? Failing this, absurdity and atheism gape behind him' (pp. 163–4). The authorial comment on atheism here underlies the theism implicit in Fred's point of view, and in his laziness and egoism. Perhaps the most damning example of a character believing in Providence is Rosamond, who 'had a Providence of her own who had kindly made her more charming than other girls, and who seemed to have arranged Fred's illness and Mr Wrench's mistake in order to bring her and Lydgate within effective proximity' (p. 297). 'What happens' confounds the expectations of all these characters.

However, it is in the portrayal of Bulstrode that many of the issues raised by this discussion are given full expression. The downfall of this upright evangelical banker of Middlemarch takes place through a chain of events that is close to melodrama in its level of coincidence. Raffles, the stepfather of Joshua Rigg, happens also to be the person who knew Bulstrode most intimately years before. While visiting his stepson in order to ask for money, he picks up a piece of paper to secure his brandy-flask in its case, and that piece of paper happens to be a letter signed by Bulstrode. Raffles's repeated visits, his alcoholism and his taunting, act as a nightmare of visitation to Bulstrode; the information that he has, and then the manner of his death, threaten Bulstrode with an unmasking that comes to pass. Like many 'sensation' novels popular in the 1860s and 1870s, *Middlemarch* shows the past intruding in an unwelcome and most tangible form on the present life of a wrong-doer: 'as if by some hideous magic, this loud red figure had risen before him in unmanageable solidity – an incorporate past which had not entered into his imagination of chastisements' (pp. 567–8). Events in Bulstrode's story occur relatively swiftly for this novel, and the features – a lost daughter, an inheritance gone astray, a haunting past – are melodramatic in character. Raffles himself comments on the coincidental and improbable train of events when he taunts Bulstrode: '"I'm not so surprised at seeing you, old fellow, because I picked up a letter – what you may call a providential thing"' (pp. 566–7). It is as if George Eliot herself is drawn to explore different modes of narrative in her exploration of what makes what happens happen.

Yet 'what happens' to Bulstrode – his torments at the hands of Raffles, his social disgrace – is less important than the examination of a particular frame of mind that he affords the reader. His interpretation and explanation of his life is egoistical: 'it was as genuinely his mode of explaining events as any theory of yours may be, if you happen to disagree with him. For the egoism which enters into our theories does not affect their sincerity; rather, the more our egoism is satisfied, the more robust is our belief' (p. 565). That mode of interpretation is ruled by his religious bent as well as by his egoism: Bulstrode is a complex study of the worldly and the spiritual, the selfish and the reverent. Like many of the other characters, he attributes what happens to Providence. For as long as this is convenient, and his life goes forward as prosperously and as happily as he wishes, Providence is an unproblematic concept. It has, indeed, allowed him to interpret those events in the past

– his involvement with somewhat disreputable pawnbroking, his marriage and suppression of his wife's daughter's existence – in a sophistical manner, arguing to himself that his worldly gain must be part of the divine plan. However, when Raffles reappears, the divine plan seems to have gone awry, and Bulstrode finds himself tortured by a consideration of motives, ends, intentions and effects. In the uncertain hours before Raffles dies, Bulstrode is forced to consider his urgent desire that Raffles's death be part of the divine plan, and to recognize that this desire is purely selfish:

his mind was intensely at work thinking of what he had to guard against and what would win him security. Whatever prayers he might lift up, whatever statements he might inwardly make of this man's wretched spiritual condition, and the duty he himself was under to submit to the punishment divinely appointed for him rather than to wish for evil to another – through all this effort to condense words into a solid mental state, there pierced and spread with irresistible vividness the images of the events he desired . . . Should Providence in this case award death, there was no sin in contemplating death as the desirable issue – if he kept his hands from hastening it – if he scrupulously did what was prescribed . . . But of course intention was everything in the question of right and wrong. (pp. 757–8)

In the end, while Bulstrode does not deliberately cause Raffles's death by contradicting Lydgate's instructions, he does succumb to his house-keeper's innocent temptation and hand the keys of his wine-cooler to her. At this point, Bulstrode is in a state of moral confusion.

George Eliot portrays Bulstrode with compassion, and is emphatic that he should not be dismissed by the reader as a mere hypocrite:

There may be coarse hypocrites, who consciously affect beliefs and emotions for the sake of gulling the world, but Bulstrode was not one of them. He was simply a man whose desires had been stronger than his theoretic beliefs, and who had gradually explained the gratification of his desires into satisfactory agreement with those beliefs. If this be hypocrisy, it is a process which shows itself occasionally in us all. (p. 667)

Yet he is condemned in his worldly and literal attempt to make restitution to Ladislaw, hoping thereby to appease some divine judge. He is also condemned by comparison with the memory of Sarah Dun-kirk's rejection of her father's means of acquiring wealth, and by Caleb Garth's unswerving decision that he has no wish to be associated with a wrong-doer such as Bulstrode.

The potential evils of a strictly religious dependence on Providence are revealed in Bulstrode. The fleeting reference to Flavell, quoted earlier, shows that George Eliot is well aware of current criticisms of sternly evangelical doctrine: the tendency to read one's own interests as God's plan, the temptation to selfishness and sophistry, the severe collision of spiritual and material interests. Bulstrode is the focus of her discussion of religion in *Middlemarch*.

In Bulstrode's experience of the past, George Eliot rewrites a providential plot so that it becomes an evolutionary plot demonstrating the law of consequences. Bulstrode has been selective in his memories. Yet when he realizes the future consequences of Raffles's return, he becomes enmeshed in the past:

The terror of being judged sharpens the memory: it sends an inevitable glare over that long-unvisited past which has been habitually recalled only in general phrases. Even without memory, the life is bound into one by a zone of dependence in growth and decay: but intense memory forces a man to own his blameworthy past. With memory set smarting like a reopened wound, a man's past is not simply a dead history, an outworn preparation of the present: it is not a repented error shaken loose from the life: it is a still quivering part of himself, bringing shudders and bitter flavours and the tinglings of a merited shame.

Into this second life Bulstrode's past had now risen, only the pleasures of it seeming to have lost their quality. Night and day, without interruption save of brief sleep which only wove retrospect and fear into a fantastic present, he felt the scenes of his earlier life coming between him and everything else, as obstinately as when we look through the window from a lighted room, the objects we turn our backs on are still before us, instead of the grass and the trees. The successive events inward and outward were there in one view: though each might be dwelt on in turn, the rest still kept their hold in the consciousness. (p. 663)

Bulstrode is forced to admit the power of the past, a power that is there in biology and geology, in 'a zone of dependence in growth and decay'. The painful resurgence of his past into his present is shown in the compelling image of the reflection of objects behind one in the window-pane of a lighted room. Thus, in looking out and forward, Bulstrode finds that he cannot dispel or ignore the events behind him. In his case, regaining a wholeness of his life in time is a nightmarish experience, the grotesque opposite of, say, the sense of wholeness in the lives of Fred and Mary.

Some comfort is given to Bulstrode by the author when his downfall becomes the occasion for Mrs Bulstrode to stand by him in affection and sympathy. She is able to put aside her own suffering to support him:

The man whose prosperity she had shared through nearly half a life, and who had unvaryingly cherished her – now that punishment had befallen him it was not possible to her in any sense to forsake him. There is a forsaking which still sits at the same board and lies on the same couch with the forsaken soul, withering it the more by unloving proximity. She knew, when she locked her door, that she should unlock it ready to go down to her unhappy husband and espouse his sorrow, and say of his guilt, I will mourn and not reproach. (p. 807)

The alternative to Mrs Bulstrode's action, 'withering ... the more by unloving proximity', is reminiscent of Rosamond's reactions to her husband's disgraces; Mrs Bulstrode's stifling of her own pain resembles Dorothea's triumphant resolution.

As the reader reaches this late stage of the novel, the various plots and characters tend to come together, and even merge. And it is these features – Bulstrode's comfort, the resonant echoes of Rosamond and Dorothea in Mrs Bulstrode's actions – that reveal the power of the author in *Middlemarch*'s world without God. Not only is the authorial voice, as every reader soon recognizes, pervasive and at times dominant, but the challenges of plot and structure, of time and space, therefore, also demand the presence of a prevailing consciousness that will direct and organize the subject-matter.

'What happens' may not be providential, may be evolutionary, according to the logic of the novel and its plots, but in another sense, 'what happens' is not accidental, for it is created by the author. Bulstrode is given some comfort; Fred Vincy achieves a wife and a way of life that suit him very well; Dorothea is rewarded for her selflessness with Ladislaw; Lydgate becomes a physician with an excellent practice and writes a treatise on gout. All outcomes have been carefully prepared for through character, action and environment within the novel, yet ultimately it is George Eliot who originates and directs the chains of cause and effect; as Peter Garrett states, she 'becomes the "Providence" her irony attempts to dissolve'.

Yet while the author's omniscience and omnipotence recall God, George Eliot remains both a scientist and a humanist in her authorial role. One of the powers that she willingly assumes may be seen if we return to a statement that has already been quoted:

In watching effects, if only of an electric battery, it is often necessary to change our place and examine a particular mixture or group at some distance from the point where the movement we are interested in was set up. The group I am moving towards is at Caleb Garth's breakfast-table ... (p. 434)

The author here decides that it is 'necessary to change our place' and to move from Mr Brooke to Caleb Garth. She steps forward to direct the course of her novel and the reader's attention. This movement performs part of the organizing and linking of strands of plot that will be discussed more fully in the following section. However, in addition, this passage demonstrates a major revision of the author as God, Providence, or originator: the author is also a scientist. The metaphor here, of 'an electric battery', proposes that the watching of effects is akin to the activity of the experimenter, an activity that suggests an open-endedness that contradicts the notion of providential design. Rosemary Ashton says, 'If a theory of art can be deduced from George Eliot's writings, it includes a view of the creative imagination as linked to the imaginative activity of the observing scientist.' There are many references to scientific observation and experimentation in *Middlemarch*. A striking example occurs when Mrs Cadwallader's movements are being described:

Even with a microscope directed on a water-drop we find ourselves making interpretations which turn out to be rather coarse; for whereas under a weak lens you may seem to see a creature exhibiting an active voracity into which other smaller creatures actively play as if they were so many animated tax-pennies, a stronger lens reveals to you certain tiniest hairlets which make vortices for these victims while the swallower waits passively at his receipt of custom. In this way, metaphorically speaking, a strong lens applied to Mrs Cadwallader's match-making will show a play of minute causes producing what may be called thought and speech vortices to bring her the sort of food she needed. (p. 83)

Here, the author observes through her microscope, and Mrs Cadwallader becomes, by analogy, a creature under scientific observation.

The description of Lydgate's research methodology is often interpreted by readers as a paradigm of George Eliot's own authorial practice:

Fever had obscure conditions, and gave him that delightful labour of the imagination which is not mere arbitrariness, but the exercise of disciplined power – combining and constructing with the clearest eye for probabilities and the fullest obedience to knowledge; and then, in yet more energetic alliance with impartial Nature, standing aloof to invent tests by which to try its own work. (pp. 193–4)

Disciplined imagination, obedience and objectivity; the willingness to test hypotheses – these may all stand for George Eliot's authorial mission. In the absence of a central 'divine' consciousness, she places at the forefront of her novel the dedication and commitment of an imaginative scientist, in the figure of Lydgate. He represents, among so many other things, the possibility of a humanist and scientific vision of existence; his aims resemble her interests.

he wanted to pierce the obscurity of those minute processes which prepare human misery and joy, those invisible thoroughfares which are the first lurking-places of anguish, mania, and crime, that delicate poise and transition which determine the growth of happy or unhappy consciousness. (p. 194)

3. The Multiplot Novel

Just as the novel as a literary form has a linear imperative of plot and character development through time, as we have seen in the discussion of 'causation' and 'coincidence', so it also has spatial imperatives, involving theme, metaphor, and unity. These are particular concerns when the novel under discussion has multiple narratives, as *Middlemarch* has. The multiplot novel is perhaps the predominant form of the novel in the mid nineteenth century. Dickens, Thackeray, Eliot and Trollope all became adept at meeting its challenges. With a number of plots and stories, a proliferation of characters, and the consequent breadth of the fiction, questions of consistency, the relation between the parts, and overall structure arise.

There also develops an emphasis on the social, on the life of the individual within a society. The terms, 'linear' and 'spatial', may, therefore, also be translated into the categories of the personal or psychological interest of the novel, and its social dimension. When reading a Victorian multiplot novel, we may be reminded of famous Victorian paintings such as *Derby Day* or *The Railway Station* by William Powell Frith, exhibited in the 1850s and 1860s; the canvas is crammed with lively representatives of almost every stratum of Victorian society. Frequently, to the reader or viewer, there is an initial sense of muddle, swiftly followed by a divination of order. We might say that a muddled society, or even a muddled universe, has been ordered, explicated, sometimes celebrated, by the author or painter. Similarly, in the journalism of Henry Mayhew, who was writing in the 1850s, we read of a popular type of exhibition called 'Happy Families': 'assemblages of animals of diverse habits and propensities living amicably, or at least quietly, in one cage'.[7] These would be exhibited at various pitches in London to the public. The fascination was in the taming of predatory impulses and the achievement of harmony, in, therefore, the triumph over evolutionary struggle and in the affirmation of a social ideal.

Like the paintings, and like 'Happy Families', the multiplot novel conveys both a panorama of social life and a harmonious ideal of that social life. Indeed, descriptive terms such as 'pictorial' or 'panoramic' have often been used in criticism, expressing both the range of subject-matter and the presence of an ordering viewer. In a highly influential review of *Middlemarch*, Henry James used these terms:

Her novel is a picture – vast, swarming, deep-coloured, crowded with episodes, with vivid images, with lurking master-strokes, with brilliant passages of expression; and as such we may freely accept it and enjoy it. It is not compact, doubtless; but when was a panorama compact?[8]

More recently, Peter Garrett has said that 'The most important possibility and primary function of multiple narrative is clearly inclusiveness.'

While the multiplot novel may demonstrate a desire to include and unite human beings within a society, it also derives some of its features from the circumstances of serial publication, so popular in the nineteenth century. Dickens, often described as a 'social' novelist in his portrayal of nineteenth-century city life, developed multiple plotting in, especially, *Bleak House*, *Little Dorrit* and *Our Mutual Friend*. More than any other novelist, he exploited and enjoyed the demands of serial publication, and multiplot novels were in one sense caused by this mode of reaching the reading public. A novel appearing over nineteen or twenty months, as Dickens's longer novels did, was bound to be long and complex, and to bear certain features: plotting to maintain his audience's interest, the interweaving of destinies of unlikely characters and overarching symbolism.

Middlemarch was composed by George Eliot at a time when Dickens's career had virtually ended: his health was failing and the only novel by him to post-date *Middlemarch* is the unfinished *Mystery of Edwin Drood*. And while Dickens characteristically writes of the fragmentation yet connectedness of London life, Eliot chooses a rural community. *Middlemarch* was not originally conceived as either a serial or a multi-plot novel. It was when George Eliot decided to combine the stories of Lydgate and Dorothea that she realized the scale of her work, and G. H. Lewes shortly afterwards suggested a form of serial publication. The panoramic spread that her themes offered was already implicit in her choice of title: *Middlemarch* was to be 'A Study of Provincial Life'. Serialization, then, was adopted after the novel was begun, but its particular demands helped to organize the structure and unity of the novel from Book III onwards.

In choosing 'provincial' life, George Eliot is drawing on a number of cultural assumptions. There is a sense of community, as Raymond Williams notes in *The Country and the City*:

it is still often said, under the pressure of urban and metropolitan experience, and as a direct and even conventional contrast, that a country community, most typically a village, is an epitome of direct relationships: of face-to-face contacts within which we can find and value the real substance of personal relationships. Certainly this immediate aspect of its difference from the city or the suburb is important; it is smaller in scale; people are more easily identified and connected within it; the structure of the community is in many ways more visible.

As a multiplot novel, *Middlemarch* aims to span the social classes, portraying many different characters and including them in a notion of community, while at the same time revealing the divisions and lack of connection between them. W. J. Harvey says, 'Certainly *Middlemarch* is, in one sense, panoramic; that is to say, if one wants to find a unifying centre, one does better to locate it in a society, in Middlemarch itself, rather than in any one individual.' But the notion of community brings with it several problems. A harmonious rural community has only ever been an idealistic and nostalgic image (usually for town-dwellers) and, as Raymond Williams observes, 'In the village as in the city there is division of labour, there is the contrast of social position, and then necessarily there are alternative points of view.' The very pressure towards ordering and patterning betrays an underlying in-security about 'society' and 'community': they were disintegrating, and the universe was not as explicable to the Victorians as they might have wished. Similarly, the carefully constructed and interwoven multiplot novel can easily be experienced as a jumble, as Henry James was inclined to see it. The issues of community and division, inclusiveness and compactness, are ways of talking about similar dilemmas in the multiplot novel; there is a pressure towards a thematic unity within the novel, and there is also an artistic imperative to impose coherence and structure. At the same time, the breadth of the novel and its subject produces diversity, difference and variety. *Middlemarch*, placed histor-ically by the author in the turbulent times up to but before the 1832 Reform Act, and aiming to convey both inclusiveness and difference, is sited at the centre of these contradictions.

Like the all-seeing painter, who orders his or her spatial effects, George Eliot is a controlling and overseeing authorial presence in her novel. She marshals information and insights into the characters, and generalizes at many points in the novel. The most famous intervention in this respect is at the beginning of Chapter 27:

An eminent philosopher among my friends, who can dignify even your ugly furniture by lifting it into the serene light of science, has shown me this pregnant little fact. Your pier-glass or extensive surface of polished steel made to be rubbed by a housemaid, will be minutely and multitudinously scratched in all directions; but place now against it a lighted candle as a centre of illumination, and lo! the scratches will seem to arrange themselves in a fine series of concentric circles round that little sun. It is demonstrable that the scratches are going everywhere impartially, and it is only your candle which produces the flattering illusion of a concentric arrangement, its light falling with an exclusive optical selection. These things are a parable. The scratches are events, and the candle is the egoism of any person now absent . . . (p. 297)

Here, the extensive psychological exploration of characters is suspended temporarily and the author steps to the centre of the reader's attention: the example of the polished pier-glass is given, apparently apropos of nothing. Once again, as we have seen in the previous section, the example is given a quasi-scientific slant with the reference to 'the serene light of science'. It is a 'pregnant little fact', we are told, and 'These things are a parable': they are a way of reading the similarities of situation and theme in the novel, calling upon a skill on the part of the reader to relate parable to immediate subject. Primarily, they are a way of uniting the novel in the reader's mind, on this occasion around the concept of egoism.

The authorial voice, then, frequently points out the connections between the stories, in an effort to link them thematically. Yet at times the very theme of egoism works to counteract statements. George Eliot is interested in showing her readers the different points of view of each individual, as for example in the following passage:

One morning, some weeks after her arrival at Lowick, Dorothea – but why always Dorothea? Was her point of view the only possible one with regard to this marriage? I protest against all our interest, all our effort at understanding being given to the young skins that look blooming in spite of trouble; for these too will get faded, and will know the older and more eating griefs which we are helping to neglect. In spite of the blinking eyes and white moles objectionable to Celia, and the want of muscular curve which was morally painful to Sir James, Mr Casaubon had an intense consciousness within him, and was spiritually a-hungered like the rest of us. (p. 312)

The authorial voice produces an overall control, and directs the reader strongly, especially in phrases such as 'we are helping to neglect', and 'like the rest of us'. Yet the determined shift away from Dorothea's story and towards Casaubon's feelings creates disruption, and this is confirmed in the passage by the parenthetical references to Celia's and Sir James's points of view. The authorial voice is here introducing a range of disagreeing voices: in the words of the Russian critic, Mikhail Bakhtin, a 'plurality of independent and unmerged voices and consciousnesses'.

The reader coming to *Middlemarch* for the first time often experiences some bewilderment precisely because of the tensions between unified structure and diversity. The most obvious, and radical, disjunction comes at the end of Chapter 10, when we lose sight of Dorothea and are asked to turn our sympathetic attention towards a gallery of new characters. Until that point, we have been reading a story about one young woman and her decision to marry. There was a practical cause for this disruption, in that the first nine or ten chapters were the fiction 'Miss Brooke', which George Eliot commenced as an independent story, and then decided to unite with the projected novel about Lydgate and the Vincys. But some critics have argued strongly for a logic in this disruption, stating that George Eliot is not here faltering in her structure. The shift from Dorothea forces the reader to contemplate another character's point of view, a procedure that is to gain momentum, and at the beginning of Chapter 11 Lydgate is linked both circumstantially and thematically back to Dorothea and forwards to Rosamond:

Lydgate, in fact, was already conscious of being fascinated by a woman strikingly different from Miss Brooke: he did not in the least suppose that he had lost his balance and fallen in love but he had said of that particular woman, 'She is grace itself; she is perfectly lovely and accomplished. That is what a woman ought to be: she ought to produce the effect of exquisite music.' Plain women he regarded as he did the other severe facts of life, to be faced with philosophy and investigated by science. But Rosamond Vincy seemed to have the true melodic charm ... (p. 121)

Already, in these few lines, Lydgate's flawed response to women is revealed. And structurally, his presence has been prepared for in Chapter 10, when he attends the dinner to celebrate Dorothea's impending marriage. There, the focus has moved from Dorothea to a number of characters, each with their own point of view. Despite the jolt for the reader, then, it is possible to argue that in Chapters 10 and 11 continuity is maintained by authorial linking, by thematic concentration on marriage and relations between men and women, and by structural emphasis on different viewpoints.

George Eliot herself held strong views about organic unity in art, and the concept of 'organic unity' appears as an emphasis in other fields such as the study of societies, as well, as has already been seen. In 'Notes on Form in Art', an essay which was never published, but which she wrote in 1868, the year before she began *Middlemarch*, she says:

the outline defining the wholeness of the human body is due to a consensus or constant interchange of effects among its parts. It is wholeness not merely of mass but of strict & manifold dependence. The word consensus expresses that fact in a complex organism by which no part can suffer increase or diminution without a participation of all other parts in the effect produced & a consequent modification of the organism as a whole.

By this light, forms of art can be called higher or lower only on the same principle as that on which we apply these words to organisms . . .

With this metaphor of the human body, George Eliot is emphasizing an organicist theory of art deriving from the ideas of the German Romantics. There are, in general, five stories in *Middlemarch*: Dorothea and Casaubon and Ladislaw, Lydgate and Rosamond, Fred Vincy and the Garths, Bulstrode, and Featherstone. They are distanced and interwoven, with varying degrees of success, in a way also described in 'Notes on Form in Art': *Middlemarch* could be called a whole 'composed of parts more & more multiplied & highly differenced, yet more & more absolutely bound together by various conditions of common likeness or mutual dependence'. This is partly achieved by the authorial voice, but a range of other techniques is also employed.

In Chapters 23 and 26, for example, Fred Vincy's debts accumulate as he makes a series of unwise decisions about buying and selling horses. He is forced to confess to the Garths, for Caleb Garth has signed a supporting note for him, and the debt has now to be paid, at the expense of the Garths, who can ill afford it. He then has to tell Mary Garth at Stone Court, and to face her distress and her inability to forgive him outright:

'I wouldn't have hurt you so for the world, Mary,' he said at last. 'You can never forgive me.'

'What does it matter whether I forgive you?' said Mary passionately. 'Would that make it any better for my mother to lose the money she has been earning by lessons for four years, that she might send Alfred to Mr Hanmer's? Should you think all that pleasant enough if I forgave you?' (p. 286)

But Mary does not altogether forget her affection for Fred, for later:

At Fred's last words she felt an instantaneous pang, something like what a mother feels at the imagined sobs or cries of her naughty truant child, which may lose itself and get harm. And when, looking up, her eyes met his dull despairing glance, her pity for him surmounted her anger and all her other anxieties. (p. 287)

After this interview, Fred is afflicted with typhoid fever, a result of his loitering in the back-streets of Houndsley, trading horses, but also as a kind of poetic justice. Fred's lesson that optimism and essential goodwill are not sufficient, his thoughtlessness, and his entanglement in money problems, all foreshadow Lydgate's later predicament. Lydgate prepares for marriage:

in an episodic way, very much as he gave orders to his tailor for every requisite of perfect dress, without any notion of being extravagant. On the contrary, he would have despised any ostentation of expense; . . . But it had never occurred to him that he should live in any other than what he would have called an ordinary way, with green glasses for hock, and excellent waiting at table. (p. 382)

Lydgate's accumulating debts force him, like Fred, to face material facts; they lead to his profound professional self-compromise, and to a confrontation with Rosamond. But there is an ironic parallel between Fred and Lydgate here. Whereas Mary's concern for her parents overrides her affection for Fred, and eventually leads Fred into a life of greater consideration for others, Rosamond's reaction is a concern for herself that overrides everything else. Lydgate appeals for her support as his wife:

'I took pains to keep it from you while you were not well; but now we must think together about it, and you must help me.'

'What can *I* do, Tertius?' said Rosamond, turning her eyes on him again. That little speech of four words, like so many others in all languages, is capable by varied vocal inflexions of expressing all states of mind from helpless dimness to exhaustive argumentative perception, from the completest self-devoting fellowship to the most neutral aloofness. Rosamond's thin utterance threw into the words 'What can *I* do!' as much neutrality as they could hold. (p. 640)

Thus the thematic parallel of money, and of the way that material concerns cannot be ignored, is twinned with an ironic investigation of the duties of marriage, and, more importantly, of sympathy with others. We may be reminded of other passages in the novel, dealing with other characters, such as Sir James's memory of 'Dorothea stretching her tender arm under her husband's neck and looking at him with unspeakable sorrow' (p. 319), and Dorothea's subsequent reaction to Lydgate's news that Casaubon may die suddenly:

There was silence for a few moments, while Dorothea sat as if she had been turned to marble, though the life within her was so intense that her mind had never before swept in brief time over an equal range of scenes and motives.

'Help me, pray,' she said, at last, in the same low voice as before. 'Tell me what I can do.' (p. 323)

Dorothea's impulse of sympathy towards her husband resembles Lydgate's fateful emotion towards Rosamond which seals their engagement:

Lydgate, forgetting everything else, completely mastered by the outrush of tenderness at the sudden belief that this sweet young creature depended on him for her joy, actually put his arms round her, folding her gently and protectingly – he was used to being gentle with the weak and suffering – and kissed each of the two large tears. (p. 336)

We may even remember these scenes and their various implications when we learn of Mrs Bulstrode's reaction to her husband's disgrace:

as she went towards him she thought he looked smaller – he seemed so withered and shrunken. A movement of new compassion and old tenderness went through her like a great wave, and putting one hand on his which rested on the arm of the chair, and the other on his shoulder, she said, solemnly but kindly –

'Look up, Nicholas.'

He raised his eyes with a little start and looked at her half amazed for a moment: her pale face, her changed, mourning dress, the trembling about her mouth, all said, 'I know'; and her hands and eyes rested gently on him. He burst out crying and they cried together, she sitting at his side. (pp. 807–8)

All these passages rely for their echoing effect on the recurrent vocabulary of tears, tenderness, gentleness and of eyes meeting. The reactions of Mary, Dorothea and Mrs Bulstrode serve to underline Rosamond's failure to respond to her husband, and the story of Rosamond and Lydgate cannot be read without such references to the other stories. In the long and intense experience of reading *Middlemarch*, we accumulate echoes and parallels that direct our attention to the themes of the novel, and that link characters in an organic whole.

Another example of 'common likeness or mutual dependence', which deals with different characters and themes, commences with the death and funeral of Featherstone, in Chapters 32 to 35. The hopeful relatives gather, all 'Waiting for Death', as the title of the Book makes clear, but they are forced to leave Mary to stay with Featherstone. On the night that he dies, as she sits with him, he asks her to destroy his second will, which she refuses to do. Of the funeral, George Eliot remarks,

We are all of us imaginative in some form or other, for images are the brood of desire; and poor old Featherstone, who laughed much at the way in which others cajoled themselves, did not escape the fellowship of illusion. In writing the programme for his burial he certainly did not make clear to himself that his pleasure in the little drama of which it formed a part was confined to anticipation. In chuckling over the vexations he could inflict by the rigid clutch of his dead hand, he inevitably mingled his consciousness with that livid stagnant presence ... (p. 358)

The following chapter reveals the true contents of Featherstone's will:

Fred has not inherited the estate, and indeed, a strange newcomer has been brought into the Middlemarch scene. Fred is

> too utterly depressed. Twenty-four hours ago he had thought that instead of needing to know what he should do, he should by this time know that he needed to do nothing: that he should hunt in pink, have a first-rate hunter, ride to cover on a fine hack, and be generally respected for doing so; moreover, that he should be able at once to pay Mr Garth, and that Mary could not longer have any reason for not marrying him. And all this was to have come without study or other inconvenience, purely by the favour of providence in the shape of an old gentleman's caprice. But now, at the end of twenty-four hours, all those firm expectations were upset. (pp. 376–7)

Fred's faith in Providence is shown to be an absurd faith in what amounts to 'an old gentleman's caprice': the irony of such a confident world-view has already been discussed. The general situation bears many similarities to another of the novel's stories. Featherstone waits for death, as do his relatives, but at this stage of the novel, Casaubon has already suffered his first attack, and Lydgate has already told Dorothea that his death may be sudden. The phrase describing Featherstone's comic imaginativeness about his funeral, 'the rigid clutch of his dead hand', prefigures the title of Book V, 'The Dead Hand', which specifically refers to Casaubon's own scandalous will. Featherstone wishes to dictate to others after his death by summoning them all to a grand funeral, and through his will he also shocks and disappoints all the hopeful relatives. Casaubon, too, cherishes the delusion that he can influence events after his death. He attempts to extract from Dorothea an undertaking that she will complete his life's work, asking her, as Featherstone asks Mary, in the watches of the night:

> he had come at last to create a trust for himself out of Dorothea's nature: she could do what she resolved to do: and he willingly imagined her toiling under the fetters of a promise to erect a tomb with his name upon it. (Not that Mr Casaubon called the future volumes a tomb; he called them the Key to all Mythologies.) But the months gained on him and left his plans belated: he had only had time to ask for that promise by which he sought to keep his cold grasp on Dorothea's life. (p. 535)

The 'cold grasp' is, however, a more sinister attempt to exert power than Featherstone's wishes were. Mary's trial with Featherstone is paralleled by Dorothea's dilemma about whether to agree to Casaubon's request, but Dorothea is rescued from her impending commitment, not by strength of will, but by Casaubon's sudden death. In *his* will, he forbids Dorothea to marry Ladislaw, on pain of losing his estates. But while Fred loses the estates he was never to have inherited, Dorothea willingly gives hers up when she is finally united with Ladislaw. Once again, these two stories are very tightly linked by the repetition of phrases, as has been seen, and by the introduction of a stranger from outside. Rigg is summoned to Middlemarch by Featherstone's death, with all the repercussions for various characters that that entails, and Ladislaw is drawn into the life of Middlemarch by the very determination of Casaubon to exclude him. Like Rigg, Ladislaw will change the lives of some of the Middlemarch characters.

Middlemarch is, then, structured and unified by techniques of parallelling and imagery, by overarching themes and an omniscient author, and by directive Book titles and parables. Whether or not this is fully consistent must be decided by the individual reader. It is just as important to note the variety and differences in the novel, differences often emphasized by the prevailing ironic tone of the novel. And, finally, there is no one agreement about *Middlemarch* and its multiple narratives. Mark Schorer says, 'here we have a work of widely diffused story materials with very little effort to tie them together by mechanical plot means, and at the same time a novel that creates a powerful effect of unity'.[9] In *Darwin's Plots*, Gillian Beer says,

Middlemarch is a work that draws attention to its own organization ... But the process of reading leads into divergence and variability. Even while we are observing how closely human beings conform in the taxonomy of event we learn how differently they feel and think. For Dorothea and Casaubon waiting for death means something very different from what it means for Mary Garth and Featherstone. The *relations* are different. The distances between people are different.

Critics have even reached opposing views about the general drift of George Eliot's technique. Barbara Hardy says that George Eliot 'makes this formal pattern say insistently that human beings are very like each other',[10] while W. J. Harvey claims that 'what emerges is not so much a theme as a set of variations'. But it was Henry James who reached the most decided and controversial conclusion, in his early review: '*Middlemarch* is a treasure-house of detail, but it is an indifferent whole'.

4. The Fabric of Quotation

Middlemarch is a novel with several main characters who are avid readers and students. Casaubon the scholar lives his life among books, and Lydgate's vocation came to him while he was browsing in his guardian's library as a boy:

one vacation, a wet day sent him to the small home library to hunt once more for a book which might have some freshness for him: in vain! unless, indeed, he took down a dusty row of volumes with grey-paper backs and dingy labels – the volumes of an old Cyclopaedia which he had never disturbed . . . before he got down from his chair, the world was made new to him by a presentiment of endless processes filling the vast spaces planked out of his sight by that wordy ignorance which he had supposed to be knowledge. From that hour Lydgate felt the growth of an intellectual passion. (pp. 172–3)

The Dorothea of the beginning of the novel reads widely and significantly yearns to be the helpmate of another Hooker, Milton or Pascal. In Rome, 'Young Mr Ladislaw was not at all deep himself in German writers; but very little achievement is required in order to pity another man's shortcomings' (p. 240), and he is able to pour scorn convincingly on Casaubon's research to Dorothea by referring to recent German sources which Casaubon is unequipped to read. At Stone Court, Mary Garth occupies her spare moments by reading, which Featherstone resents. Mary jokingly mediates her experience through literature, just as Dorothea draws passionate inspiration from *her* reading. Fred says to Mary,

'I suppose a woman is never in love with any one she has always known – ever since she can remember; as a man often is. It is always some new fellow who strikes a girl.'

'Let me see,' said Mary, the corners of her mouth curling archly; 'I must go back on my experience. There is Juliet – she seems an example of what you say. But then Ophelia had probably known Hamlet a long while; and Brenda Troil – she had known Mordaunt Merton ever since they were children; . . .' (p. 167)

Susan Garth, too, is proud of her scholarly powers, and teaches her younger children as she goes about her domestic duties. In a comic parallel, Mr Brooke fancies himself as something of a scholar. He tells Casaubon:

'I took in all the new ideas at one time – human perfectibility, now. But some say, history moves in circles; and that may be very well argued; I have argued it myself. The fact is, human reason may carry you a little too far – over the hedge, in fact. It carried me a good way at one time; but I saw it would not do. I pulled up; I pulled up in time. But not too hard. I have always been in favour of a little theory: we must have Thought; else we shall be landed back in the dark ages. But talking of books, there is Southey's *Peninsular War.* I am reading that of a morning.' (p. 39)

Brooke has dabbled in a range of writings and ideas, and none of them has stuck. He proceeds to ask Casaubon the most banal of questions: '"how do you arrange your documents?"' (p. 42).

Books and reading, then, are vital elements in the world of this novel, and *Middlemarch*, like many novels, is in part a meditation on the power of the word. At times it seems that, as in the portrayal of Casaubon or Brooke, George Eliot is suggesting that dedicated students may lose touch with the reality of emotion, human relationships, economic pressures, or social life. Mary and Susan Garth possess the positive ability to combine book-learning with domestic skills, but Dorothea's fervour is theoretical rather than wrought by experience (and this theme develops both into the study of sympathetic feeling that Dorothea must attain, and into the investigation of the practical possibilities for women at that time). However, at other times in the novel, those who do not enjoy reading and study, such as Fred and Rosamond Vincy, are thereby designated shallow, materialistic, or less sympathetic as characters. For example, on the first appearance of this brother and sister, Fred comes down to breakfast late, and reads a novel when he should be studying. Rosamond, after meeting Lydgate, studies more than ever to be 'her own standard of a perfect lady', and this seems to involve some application to 'good' literature: 'She found time also to read the best novels, and even the second best, and she knew much poetry by heart' (p. 196). The shallowness of her reading habits is underlined in the comical occasion when she looks over the latest *Keepsake* with her callow admirer, Ned Plymdale. To Rosamond, what one enjoys reading has no basis in intellectual pleasure, but is merely an index of good taste. On the other hand, Lydgate is arrogantly dismissive of any fiction whatsoever:

Lydgate, drawing the *Keepsake* towards him and opening it, gave a short scornful laugh and tossed up his chin, as if in wonderment at human folly ...

'I think I shall turn round on you and accuse you of being a Goth,' said Rosamond, looking at Lydgate with a smile. 'I suspect you know nothing about Lady Blessington and L.E.L.' Rosamond herself was not without relish for these writers, but she did not readily commit herself by admiration, and was alive to the slightest hint that anything was not, according to Lydgate, in the very highest taste. (pp. 303, 304)

In this thematic exploration, it is inevitable that references to specific books will be manifold in the novel. Other nineteenth-century novels, such as *Jude the Obscure* by Thomas Hardy, which deals with similar themes of education and book-learning, contain a similar range of references, although not as extensive as there exists in *Middlemarch*. But in another way, *Middlemarch* exhibits a preoccupation with the written or printed word that reflects the author's own learning and that makes it supremely textual: the texture of the writing is an evocation of other writings.

It is becoming a critical commonplace that all writing is 'intertextual', relying on past writings in both subliminal and deliberate ways. A novel, in this terminology, becomes a *text*, in which a number of statements or writings are brought together. In *Middlemarch*, the thematic focus on scholarship and the activities of many of the characters help to bring this intertextual dimension to the foreground. Just as the political aspirations of Brooke, or the business aims of Caleb Garth, are placed historically and economically by references to an historical and social context, so a wide spectrum of quotations, references and allusions is employed to encourage the reader to assess characters, interpret events, and comprehend ironies.

The generic term for such authorial activity is 'allusion'. This may be taken to include deliberate quotations which are attributed, submerged quotations which an alert reader might notice, and references to characters or events in previous literature, history or philosophy. Frequently such use of allusion exists to create a gap, often ironic, between the past and the present, between a noble past enshrined in literary and historical representations and a mundane present, between idealistic aspiration and human failing. There is, therefore, a 'play' between two levels, and the reader becomes adept at interpreting the relationship between the quoted words and the more immediate situation or character in the novel.

It seems reasonable to assume that middle-class habits in Victorian Britain of reading aloud, memorizing passages from selected texts, listening to sermons and reading devotional or religious texts exclusively on Sundays – habits which are widely documented but, of course, were by no means universal – encouraged a readership that was practised in recognizing a limited range of quotations and in interpreting the relationship between motto and explication. The Prelude in *Middlemarch*, recounting the story of Saint Theresa of Avila, and the chapter-headings, of quotations with little direct relevance to the internal world of the novel, evoke a certain reading practice. These features are not unique to George Eliot's works, but are common to the novels of many Victorian writers.

In addition to this tradition of moral and interpretive writing, some readers possessed a second set of interpretive skills, created by a common classical education (common, that is, to a predominantly white, middle-class, male section of the population). References to Latin and Greek writings would be accessible to this readership, and also many of the great 'classics' of English and European literature. At this point it is useful once again to recall George Eliot's own extensive, and intellectually adventurous, reading in philosophical, scientific and anthropological thought. There are, then, layers of writing activity enmeshed in the text of *Middlemarch*. These layers are caused by the textual dimension of all writing, by the thematic focus on books within the novel, by the customary reading skills and cultural fund of a Victorian readership, and by George Eliot's own impressive reading.

For the reader in the late twentieth century, the consideration of allusion becomes increasingly problematic as the text being read recedes further into the past. Those historical events that were relatively recent when the novel was first published, for example, are often lost or forgotten in the 1980s. So it is, too, with literary allusions. Commonly known texts, such as the Bible, the Book of Common Prayer, or *The Pilgrim's Progress* (a very widespread point of reference in Victorian fiction), with which a large section of the population was familiar in the nineteenth century, are less commonly known now. Furthermore, we cannot be confident that we know the levels of shared cultural assumptions among people in the 1870s, or more specifically, among George Eliot's readership. There is a necessary gap between *Middlemarch* in the 1870s and *Middlemarch* in the 1980s, caused by cultural and historical change. Neither can we hope to recapture the receptiveness of George Eliot's readership to her allusions because of the impossibility of defining her original readership. Nonetheless, it is important that we attempt an historical awareness of the ways in which *Middlemarch* might have been read in 1873. For example, the finer detail of Casaubon's benighted research and of Lydgate's true potential as a medical scientist, as we have seen earlier, are probably less immediately accessible to the reader now than then, but without some appreciation of George Eliot's references, we lose some of her deliberate mapping of the two characters' endeavours. Similarly, we may be unversed in the literature alluded to in the novel, but this allusiveness operates on at least two levels: a probable common culture, and a more specific culture possessed by George Eliot which was possibly shared by a certain section of her readership.

The texture of literary reference in the novel is, then, like the scientific, philosophical and historical contexts, an integral part of *Middlemarch*, eliciting certain interpretive and reading skills on our part. The novel contains a number of features that are important in this respect: the Prelude, the chapter-headings, deliberate quotations which abound in the text, and more submerged quotations which provide an undercurrent of multiple meanings for the alert, or equipped, reader.

George Eliot chooses to begin this long novel, not with the opening description of Miss Brooke in Chapter 1, but with a Prelude that discusses Saint Theresa of Avila, a nun who lived from 1515 until 1582, founded a number of convents along new lines against considerable opposition, and was canonized in 1622. In somewhat elliptical prose, that has given rise to critical disagreement about her ultimate drift, George Eliot describes Saint Theresa's vocation:

Theresa's passionate, ideal nature demanded an epic life: what were many-volumed romances of chivalry and the social conquests of a brilliant girl to her? Her flame quickly burned up that light fuel; and, fed from within, soared after some illimitable satisfaction, some object which would never justify weariness, which would reconcile self-despair with the rapturous consciousness of life beyond self. She found her epos in the reform of a religious order. (p. 25)

There are many ideas here: the existence of a certain kind of personality that is 'passionate' and 'ideal', the reasonable but comparatively second-rate alternatives for most girls, of chivalric romance or 'social conquests', the striving for an almost indescribable fulfilment, and the mundane preoccupations of 'self' that such a fulfilment would vanquish. Already, the reader who comes to the novel for the first time will be aware that he or she is being required to contemplate an unusual state of existence: literally, the stuff that saints are made of. The reader who already knows the novel will be reminded not only of Dorothea's own 'passionate, ideal nature', but also of the stain of self that, in different ways and to different degrees, sullies the vocations of Lydgate and Casaubon. Saint Theresa is not mentioned further, but her situation, as described by the author, becomes the opportunity for an extended comparison between her and similar young women in contemporary times. George Eliot provides us with a list of hindrances to the aspirations of later Theresas. Life is no longer 'epic'; 'meanness of opportunity' may have led to a rather bungled life, or to tragic failure; there is a lack of 'coherent social faith and order' which might have provided a framework for action. She raises the question that such 'blundering lives' are the result of a stereotypical female indecisiveness, but appears to dismiss this possibility, suggesting instead that 'the social lot of women' might have something to do with it. The Prelude ends with two examples of tragic alienation for the kind of personality that has been described:

Here and there a cygnet is reared uneasily among the ducklings in the brown pond, and never finds the living stream in fellowship with its own oary-footed kind. Here and there is born a Saint Theresa, foundress of nothing, whose loving heart-beats and sobs after an unattained goodness tremble off and are dispersed among hindrances, instead of centring in some long-recognizable deed. (p. 26)

Immediately, then, before we have met any of the characters of the novel, we have been provided with a way of 'reading' Dorothea as a latter-day Saint Theresa whose lack of an arena for action causes both comic and tragic outcomes. We have also been introduced to the notion of failure: failure which is caused by a myriad of factors. The initial historical reference has obliquely *and* explicitly laid down some of the central themes of the novel. After we have finished *Middlemarch*, we may return to the Prelude and ask whether it is, in fact, wholly programmatic of what is to follow, or if, on the contrary, Dorothea's 'failure' has been a success: a question that the Finale itself raises and attempts, not always satisfactorily, to answer. The critical disagreement, caused partly by the shifts in tone in the Prelude, is about whether Dorothea should be regarded as a wholly sympathetic character in the opening pages of the novel, or if, on the other hand, gentle ridicule prevails.

Not only does the Prelude provide a paradigm for considering Dorothea and other characters, but it also exhibits in its linguistic texture a number of metaphoric allusions to other aspects of the novel that is to follow. The grandly rolling sentence that opens the Prelude immediately introduces the concepts of history and time: 'Who that cares much to know the history of man, and how the mysterious mixture behaves under the varying experiments of Time, has not dwelt, at least briefly, on the life of Saint Theresa' (p. 25). The word 'varying' here is picked up again towards the end of the Prelude, but with particular allusion to Darwinian theories of species:

if there were one level of feminine incompetence as strict as the ability to count three and no more, the social lot of women might be treated with scientific certitude. Meanwhile the indefiniteness remains, and the limits of variation are really much wider than any one would imagine from the sameness of women's coiffure and the favourite love-stories in prose and verse. (p. 26)

The theme of 'the social lot of women', mentioned here, has already been touched upon in the phrase, 'meanness of opportunity', which itself should alert the reader to the historical dimension of the novel. And the comment, 'a tragic failure which found no sacred poet and sank unwept into oblivion' (p. 25), ironically hints at one of the many roles of the narrator, who acts as a secular 'poet' with the final words of the novel, 'the number who lived faithfully a hidden life, and rest in unvisited tombs' (p. 896).

Each chapter is structured on a similar principle: of the eighty-six chapters, fifty-four have epigraphs taken from past writers, while thirty-two were written by George Eliot herself. A notable early example is Chapter 4. Here the epigraph is by the author:

1st Gent. Our deeds are fetters that we forge ourselves.
2nd Gent. Ay, truly: but I think it is the world
  That brings the iron. (p. 58)

In this chapter, Dorothea is enlightened by Celia as to Sir James Chettam's intentions. Her reaction is shocked distress. On her return home, Mr Brooke gives her some pamphlets sent by Mr Casaubon, which she takes

as eagerly as she might have taken in the scent of a fresh bouquet after a dry, hot, dreary walk.
   She was getting away from Tipton and Freshitt, and her own sad liability to tread in the wrong places on her way to the New Jerusalem. (p. 61)

Mr Brooke also has Casaubon's proposal of marriage to report to Dorothea, and there follows a moving discussion in which the uncle tries to persuade his niece to consider her acceptance with more leisure, but his persuasions are haphazard and vague. The epigraph points up many of the inherent ironies of the chapter: Dorothea thinks that she can see fetters in marrying Sir James, but never suspects the moment-ousness of her decision to marry Casaubon. The second gentleman's qualification is also demonstrated, in the way that social opinion and expectation push Dorothea in her suffering towards Casaubon as an apparent saviour from 'the unfriendly mediums of Tipton and Freshitt' which 'had issued in crying and red eyelids' (p. 62). The epigraph also expresses in a succinct way the whole notion of human agency, causation and event, discussed in the section on 'Causation and Coincidence'.

The epigraph to Chapter 12 is not composed by George Eliot, but is drawn from Chaucer's *Miller's Tale*, ll. 3774–5: 'He had more tow on his distaffe/Than Gerveis knew' (p. 131). The connections between epigraph and chapter are here somewhat more subterranean. In this chapter, Fred and Rosamond Vincy ride to Stone Court. Both, as the reader has already seen, have an ulterior motive: Fred has 'expectations' of Featherstone, but is also fond of Mary Garth, while Rosamond is coolly scheming to meet Lydgate for the first time. When they arrive, Fred is challenged by Featherstone to disprove the allegation that he has borrowed money on the strength of his expectations; Rosamond succeeds in meeting, and impressing, Lydgate. The epigraph is a now obsolete colloquialism, meaning, 'He had more work in hand', or 'more trouble to cause, than Gerveis knew'. It refers to the revenge meditated by Absolon, a young parish clerk, on a pair of lovers who have humiliated him. In the context of Chapter 12, then, it refers to those ulterior motives of Fred and Rosamond. But Fred's future prospects are not to come to him as easily as he would wish: Middlemarch gossip has a strength that can thwart his desires. And we might also read an ominous note into Mary's simultaneous defence and rejection of Fred to Rosamond: '"I would not marry him if he asked me"' (p. 143) – which at present he finds it easy enough to dismiss – '"She would not have said so if you had not provoked her"' (p. 148); Mary will later require considerable seriousness from Fred before she consents to marry him. Fred's plans are ironically gainsaid. The sense of someone making trouble that the epigraph conveys applies equally to Featherstone, whose challenge to Fred is a foretaste of his will, which disappoints all his relatives.

The theme gains resonance with Lydgate's experience in this chapter. In the previous chapter, which has in fact moved into a time later than the events of Chapter 12 in the story of Miss Brooke, we have been told that:

Rosamond Vincy seemed to have the true melodic charm; and when a man has seen the woman whom he would have chosen if he had intended to marry speedily, his remaining a bachelor will usually depend on her resolution rather than on his. Lydgate believed that he should not marry for several years: not marry until he had trodden out a good clear path for himself away from the broad road . . . (p. 121)

In the chapter under discussion, which moves back in time, we witness the first meeting between Lydgate and Rosamond, and it becomes even more evident that Rosamond has definite plans concerning him: she will not provide the 'resolution' that will preserve Lydgate as a bachelor. Practically the entire history of this couple is encapsulated in the description of Rosamond's thoughts as she and Fred ride home:

before they had ridden a mile she was far on in the costume and introductions of her wedded life, having determined on her house in Middlemarch, and foreseen the visits she would pay to her husband's high-bred relatives at a distance, whose finished manners she could appropriate as thoroughly as she had done her school accomplishments, preparing herself thus for vaguer elevations which might ultimately come. There was nothing financial, still less sordid, in her previsions: she cared about what were considered refinements, and not about the money that was to pay for them. (p. 146)

While, therefore, there is no inkling of the revenge so prominent in Chaucer's Tale, the epigraph underlines that Rosamond, and Featherstone, are up to no good. It also works ironically to show Fred being thwarted in his unexpressed desires.

Another example can be seen in the epigraphs to Chapters 19 and 20. Once again, these chapters display some modification of the time scheme in the novel. Chapter 19 shows Dorothea in a pensive attitude in the Vatican, and noticed by two young men, Naumann and Ladislaw; Chapter 20 begins two hours later, with Dorothea in tears in the privacy of her apartments, and then goes back to reveal the causes both of her distress and of her melancholy in the Vatican earlier. The epigraph to Chapter 19 comes from Dante's *Purgatory*, Canto vii, and may be translated: 'See the other, who has made a bed for his cheek with the palm of his hand, and sighs'. This is precisely Dorothea's stance:

one beautiful ungloved hand pillowed her cheek, pushing somewhat backward the white beaver bonnet which made a sort of halo to her face around the simply braided dark-brown hair. She was not looking at the sculpture, probably not thinking of it: her large eyes were fixed dreamily on a streak of sunlight which fell across the floor. (p. 220)

The quotation from Dante should tell us quite explicitly that Dorothea is in Purgatory, and an irony arises from the fact that she is observed as an aesthetically pleasing sight by Naumann. The ensuing conversation between Naumann and Ladislaw about the merits and function of art is brought into contrast with an intimation of spiritual pain. Chapter 20 expands on Dorothea's pain. The epigraph was composed by George Eliot:

A child forsaken, waking suddenly,

> Whose gaze afeard on all things round doth rove,
> And seeth only that it cannot see
> The meeting eyes of love.
>
> (p. 224)

This is a concise description of Dorothea's panic at the art and history of Rome, before which she is childlike, and of Casaubon's failure to console her. The imagery of sight is developed in the chapter to become one of the most memorable similes in the entire novel:

Our moods are apt to bring with them images which succeed each other like the magic-lantern pictures of a doze; and in certain states of dull forlornness Dorothea all her life continued to see the vastness of St Peter's, the huge bronze canopy, the excited intention in the attitudes and garments of the prophets and evangelists in the mosaics above, and the red drapery which was being hung for Christmas spreading itself everywhere like a disease of the retina. (p. 226)

It is a chapter of profound psychological exploration, and the roles of Casaubon and Dorothea are somewhat reversed towards the end, when Dorothea artlessly asks Casaubon if he may soon begin in the actual composition of his great work. Casaubon is also like a child in his sensitivity to criticism:

Here, towards this particular point of the compass, Mr Casaubon had a sensitiveness to match Dorothea's, and an equal quickness to imagine more than the fact. He had formerly observed with approbation her capacity for worshipping the right object; he now foresaw with sudden terror that this capacity might be replaced by presumption, this worship by the most exasperating of all criticism, – that which sees vaguely a great many fine ends and has not the least notion of what it costs to reach them. (p. 233)

Once again, the imagery of sight recurs. That the epigraph translates these emotions into those of childish panic conveys Casaubon's pettiness, in particular, but also the pathos of both characters' situations, their vulnerability and loneliness.

The epigraph to Chapter 34, composed by George Eliot, focuses on two major themes of the novel: the force of social opinion, amorphous but effective in its united front, and class divisions within a society. Dorothea, Celia, Sir James, Mrs Cadwallader, and later, Brooke and Casaubon, are together at Lowick to witness from afar the funeral of Featherstone, which is attended by, among others, the Vincy family. The epigraph says:

1st Gent. Such men as this are feathers, chips and straws,
   Carry no weight, no force.

2nd Gent.   But levity
  Is casual too, and makes the sum of weight.
  For power finds its place in lack of power;
  Advance is cession, and the driven ship
  May run aground because the helmsman's thought
  Lacked force to balance opposites. (p. 357)

The chapter emphasizes neatly the divisions in this society, where none of the spectators except for Brooke can recognize the Vincys. This does not prevent individuals from passing comments on Mr Vincy, some without personal knowledge of the man: '"a very good fellow"', says Brooke; '"A coursing fellow, though"', in Sir James's opinion; '"one of those who suck the life out of the wretched hand-loom weavers in Tipton and Freshitt"', says Mrs Cadwallader (p. 361). Here, personal, aristocratic and economic considerations all produce differing estimations. A certain disdain for the lower classes implicit in these comments is not, however, shared by Dorothea:

The country gentry of old time lived in a rarefied social air: dotted apart on their stations up the mountain they looked down with imperfect discrimination on the belts of thicker life below. And Dorothea was not at ease in the perspective and chilliness of that height. (p. 360)

The epigraph, then, directs attention to the various features of Middlemarch as a community, and the chapter touches upon Dorothea's unhappy relationship to it. In addition, the chapter itself is one of the few occasions when many characters are brought into juxtaposition. The author allows the reader an easy movement from class to class which is denied to the characters, and demonstrates both unity and division – that tension which is so characteristic of the novel in its structure and patterning.

It would be impossible to analyse the extent of quotation from other texts within the text of *Middlemarch*, for it is evident on almost every page. The degree of scientific allusion will be discussed later, and certain historical allusions have already been glossed in the section on 'History and the Novel'. It is, however, relevant at this stage to observe that, as befits students and scholars, Dorothea and Casaubon in particular are frequently associated with literature and myth. Dorothea casts Casaubon as a great man, '"remarkably like the portrait of Locke"' (p. 42), 'as instructive as Milton's "affable archangel"' (p. 46), 'a living Bossuet', and 'a modern Augustine' (p. 47). Much later her character and habits are sketched in by a description of her favourite books:

There was a little heap of them on the table in the bow-window – of various sorts, from Herodotus, which she was learning to read with Mr Casaubon, to her old companion Pascal, and Keble's *Christian Year*. But to-day she opened one after another, and could read none of them. Everything seemed dreary: the portents before the birth of Cyrus – Jewish antiquities – oh dear! (p. 515)

Cyrus the Great, founder of the Persian empire, is described in Herodotus' *History of the Greek and Persian War*, which Dorothea is reading, and which George Eliot mentions a number of times in the course of the novel. He reappears in the Finale: 'Her full nature, like that river of which Cyrus broke the strength, spent itself in channels' (p. 896). Cyrus dispersed the river Gyndes into 360 channels, in order to avert the fall of Babylon, but his strategy only succeeded for one year, a fact that George Eliot noted privately. It is from a network of minor allusions like these that the texture of quotation is built up.

Appropriately, considering his preoccupation with mythology, Casaubon is often described in imagery that evokes Hades, god of the underworld. '"He is a little buried in books"' (p. 62); to Celia, 'There was something funereal in the whole affair' (pp. 72–3), and he carries 'his taper among the tombs of the past' (p. 457). This association with death carries with it, too, a fatal sterility. During courtship, his speeches have a 'frigid rhetoric' (p. 73), and tellingly, in Rome he discounts the tale of Cupid and Psyche: '"Some of them represent the fable of Cupid and Psyche, which is probably the romantic invention of a literary period, and cannot, I think, be reckoned as a genuine mythical product"' (p. 229). The story of Cupid and Psyche tells of the marriage between the god of love and a human woman: it also signifies the union of the flesh and the spirit in love. Casaubon's dismissal of it suggests his failure to perceive its deeper significance, or to unite Cupid and Psyche in his own marriage.

Dorothea becomes Casaubon's prisoner in his world of death, just as Persephone was captured by Hades and taken to the underworld until rescued for a number of months each year through her mother's intercession, just as, too, Eurydice went to the underworld and was nearly rescued by Orpheus:

it appeared that she was to live more and more in a virtual tomb, where there was the apparatus of a ghastly labour producing what would never see the light. To-day she had stood at the door of the tomb and seen Will Ladislaw receding into the distant world of warm activity and fellowship – turning his face towards her as he went. (p. 516)

Here Ladislaw takes the role of Orpheus, who led Eurydice to the gates of the underworld, only to turn round and look at her, thereby losing her and consigning her to Hades' world.

In this chapter where Dorothea looks with ennui at her reading, and mourns the loss of Will's youth and warmth, there is a sentence, 'Books were of no use'. Dorothea is trapped in Casaubon's world of books. And perhaps the most striking aspect of the intertextuality of *Middlemarch* is the position of the author. The confident, learned, omniscient and wide-ranging authorial voice encompasses other texts, but also delegates authority to other sources of knowledge. Literature, myths, text-books abound, yet there is a residual element of ambivalence. It has been said by many critics that *Middlemarch* is about 'knowledge': the progress of knowledge and the relativity of knowledge. Through the very texture of the writing, the progress of knowledge is noted by means of references to past or superseded authorities, and the relativity of knowledge is stressed by the sheer range of quotation.

III Commentary and Analysis

1. 'A Study of Provincial Life'

The full title of the novel is *Middlemarch: A Study of Provincial Life*. In a somewhat perverse way, it is helpful first to comment on what the title is not. It is not the name of an individual, such as 'Miss Brooke'. Neither is it a description of a major theme, such as 'Great Expectations', nor a forewarning of events in the novel, such as Balzac's 'Lost Illusions' – though any of these titles would be appropriate. Like 'Mansfield Park' and 'Wuthering Heights', the title draws attention to the significance of an environment. However, 'Middlemarch' has occasionally drawn attempts from commentators to detect a symbolic resonance: the word might refer to middle age (being in the 'middle' of one's 'march' through life), or it might be an oxymoron, linking 'middle' with the contradictory word 'march' in its sense of 'boundary or border district'. These possibilities are suggestive; in particular, John F. Hulcoop offers a detailed reading of the title:

Middlemarch – a paradoxical place-name – stands for both a fictitious town in the midlands and that ever-expanding section of human society whose marches are contiguous, on the one hand, with the aristocracy, on the other, with the proletariat.

He proceeds to argue that *Middlemarch* exhibits all kinds of 'middles' – the middle-aged, the middle-class, the mediocre – and that it is presented in the 'medium' of prose, 'a major metonymy for "the prosaic neighbourhood" in which these fictitious events occur'.[1]

An approach to the novel through its title produces here a specific interpretation, involving a view of Dorothea and Lydgate as 'mediocre', and a conclusion that the novel is about disillusion and limitation. More generally, what is notable about the full title of the novel is that it proposes the topic of a town and community. Early reviewers tended to be alert to this aspect of the novel. For example, R. H. Hutton, reviewing the completed novel in the *Spectator* in December 1872, said:

The book is called 'A Study of Provincial Life', and answers to its title. Round the central characters are grouped at greater or less distance all the elements of country society – the country gentry, the surveyor, the clergymen of various types, the country doctors, the banker, the manufacturers, the shopkeepers, the coroner, the auctioneer, the veterinary surgeon, the horse-dealer, the innkeepers, all drawn with a force and yet a perspective which it takes time, and a graduation of feeling not easily commanded in the few hours usually devoted to a novel, to apprehend.

Hutton has caught the range and ambitiousness of the novel, and the attention demanded of the reader by such highly conceptualized material. He also touches on the issue of the authorial perspective implied in the subtitle. The word 'Study' suggests a claim to observe and examine in a systematic manner, bearing overtones of an academic and/or scientific approach. 'Provincial' as a term (particularly in contrast to a silent alternative, 'regional') intimates a distanced, metropolitan point of view. The term, 'Provincial Life', in addition, is so general that it displays an authorial intention to produce a comprehensive and definitive analysis of a certain way of life.

Already, then, in thinking about the meanings of the book's title, a number of issues have become apparent: the importance of environment, the possible metaphorical dimensions, the panoramic ambition, and the author's role and attitude. When we begin to consider the novel as being 'about' the town of Middlemarch, and 'about' the experience of provincial life, several aspects become prominent. There are the social dynamics of the community – people living closely together and experiencing both dependency and friction – and the differences in social class and temperament. There is the series of associations that cluster around the notion of the 'provincial': protective, tranquil and secure, Middlemarch is yet excluded from a metropolitan centre, for those of the higher classes, of power, intellectual endeavour and social activity, and can be experienced as exclusive, small-minded and limiting. There is, finally, the response of a relatively small and out-of-the-way community to national events, to change and to innovation – to history as it appears in the text-books.

Middlemarch shows the reader a considerable spectrum of social class. Sir James Chettam at Freshitt Hall, a baronet, mixes socially with Mrs Cadwallader, wife of the Rector at Freshitt, and with Mr Brooke and his nieces at Tipton Grange. Significantly, all live outside the urban centre. Casaubon, too, who enters this circle, lives outside Middlemarch, at Lowick Grange. Within the town, the Vincys and the Bulstrodes are leading lights in commerce, administration, religion and social life. Mr Vincy is a manufacturer and the newly elected mayor; Mr Bulstrode is a banker, and prominent in his piety. This milieu is the central, middle-class focus of the novel in many ways. The Garths and Featherstone, while slightly removed, are related to the Vincys by marriage. In

addition, it is through occasions such as dinners and committee meetings, presided over by Vincy and Bulstrode, that the reader meets the
professional range of medical men – Sprague, Minchin, Wrench, Toller
– and the clerics, Farebrother and Tyke. There are less frequent, but still
notable, inclusions of the lower-middle-class fraternity who congregate
at the Green Dragon, and the rather different drinkers at the Tankard
in Slaughter Lane, where Mrs Dollop rules. On a couple of occasions, a
voice is lent to those less fortunate – Dagley in his poverty, criticizing
Mr Brooke, and the farm labourers who will not accept that the
coming of the railway will be beneficial to them, despite Caleb Garth's
well-meaning persuasiveness.

The novel, then, attempts to cover many levels, and there is at once a
pressure to demonstrate organic interaction, dependency and cohesion
between the social classes, and a constant portrayal of the necessarily
different priorities and points of view. A few brief examples will be
useful here. Brooke's proprietorship of *The Pioneer* and his decision
to stand as a candidate for Reform thrust him into contact with the
people of Middlemarch in ways that he has not expected. He is
forced to reconsider his role as landlord. His speech to the electors is
disrupted by the appearance of a parodic figure that echoes his rambl-
ing comments: comic as this is, it symbolizes how Brooke cannot
distance himself from the reactions and opinions of the community.
Equally, the misinformed and impulsive opinions of Mrs Dollop and
her circle of customers do not remain ineffectual in a wider sphere:
they travel as rumour, gossip and report, playing a small but significant part in the downfalls of Lydgate and Bulstrode. The divisions
are particularly evident in comments such as that which describes the
constitution of the dinner party that Brooke gives for Dorothea and
Casaubon before their wedding: 'The Miss Vincy who had the honour
of being Mr Chichely's ideal was of course not present; for Mr
Brooke, always objecting to go too far, would not have chosen that
his nieces should meet the daughter of a Middlemarch manufacturer,
unless it were on a public occasion' (p. 116). Lydgate, almost deliberately blind to the social dynamics of a provincial community, suffers
from prejudice and resistance, but he also acts according to social distinctions:

his profession had familiarized him with all grades of poverty, and he cared
much for those who suffered hardships. He would have behaved perfectly at a
table where the sauce was served in a jug with the handle off, and he would have
remembered nothing about a grand dinner except that a man was there who

talked well. But it had never occurred to him that he should live in any other than what he would have called an ordinary way, with green glasses for hock, and excellent waiting at table. (p. 382)

Despite his sympathy for the under-privileged, and his scorn for the social pretensions of his cousins at Quallingham, then, Lydgate suffers just as much as others from a certain snobbery and class-consciousness.

The paradoxes of life within a defined community are notable in *Middlemarch*. An extended description in Chapter 11 begins, 'who of any consequence in Middlemarch was not connected or at least acquainted with the Vincys?' (p. 123). The phrase, 'of any consequence', immediately draws lines between certain circles of interaction. The passage goes on to tell how Mrs Bulstrode is Mr Vincy's sister, and Mrs Vincy's sister had been Featherstone's second wife. In Chapter 23, we are told that Mr Garth's sister had been Featherstone's first wife, thus creating a 'slight connection' between the Vincys and the Garths. Even within this intricate network of kinship, the contradictions begin to appear. Mrs Bulstrode has married an outsider 'altogether of dimly known origin' (p. 123). The Vincys have been manufacturers in Middlemarch for a long time and 'had kept a good house for three generations', but both Fred and Rosamond fret against familial and social constraints. For Fred, at the beginning,

To be born the son of a Middlemarch manufacturer, and inevitable heir to nothing in particular, while such men as Mainwaring and Vyan – certainly life was a poor business, when a spirited young fellow, with a good appetite for the best of everything, had so poor an outlook. (pp. 146–7)

Fred's rejection of his milieu is interesting for the way that, after initially aiming at visions of a higher-class life, he opts to be seen to 'go down in the world' in occupation and in marriage. For however tightly knit this particular society may be, the differences are never forgotten:

Even when Caleb Garth was prosperous, the Vincys were on condescending terms with him and his wife, for there were nice distinctions of rank in Middlemarch; and though old manufacturers could not any more than dukes be connected with none but equals, they were conscious of an inherent social superiority which was defined with great nicety in practice, though hardly expressible theoretically. (p. 263)

Even before Caleb's business failures, Mrs Garth's education has been seen as a social misfortune, especially by other women such as Mrs

Vincy, for Mrs Garth, in being educated, has been a teacher – that is, she has worked for money in the past.

'Provincialism' is a complex term, denoting both small-mindedness and contentment. Its single meaning at any point depends on the perspective from which it is viewed. Rosamond, ironically, though truly 'provincial', is strongly aware of the social disadvantages of living in the provinces. She is prettily disparaging to Lydgate about her skills and knowledge, thereby flattering him and dissociating herself from her relatives. Lydgate thinks that he sees possibilities for independence in the provinces as distinct from living and working in a great city, but he later says to Dorothea, after recounting some of his difficulties, '"the ignorance of people about here is stupendous . . . there is no stifling the offence of being young, and a new-comer, and happening to know something more than the old inhabitants"' (p. 479). Dorothea suffers greatly from the small-mindedness that exists around her, yet her experience in Rome becomes the occasion for an observation of a more general form of 'provincialism'. In her uncomprehending recoil from the art and history of Rome, she is 'a girl who had been brought up in English and Swiss Puritanism, fed on meagre Protestant histories and on art chiefly of the hand-screen sort' (p. 225). Here, Dorothea herself suffers from a frame of mind and an education that do not have the scope to allow for the strange, the different, or the unknown. Dorothea's position leads on to that area of the novel that generally debates the absence of knowledge, such as in Casaubon's ignorance of German, or Brooke's ignorance of the meaning of the information he has collected. In this context, Ladislaw is almost overwritten in the text as an 'outsider' who threatens and unsettles provincialism. He is of foreign extraction, unknown and unassimilated, and he brings news, new ideas, and new emotions to the world of Middlemarch. Consequently he attracts numerous epithets, notably from Mrs Cadwallader, that aim to marginalize him.

Rosamond, like her aunt Bulstrode, is to marry an outsider. Indeed, she is determined to, for 'a stranger was absolutely necessary to Rosamond's social romance, which had always turned on a lover and bridegroom who was not a Middlemarcher, and who had no connections at all like her own' (p. 145). Rosamond is an incurable snob, with a nose 'to discern very subtly the faintest aroma of rank' (pp. 195–6), and she 'felt that she might have been happier if she had not been the daughter of a Middlemarch manufacturer. She disliked anything which reminded her that her mother's father had been an innkeeper' (p. 128). She finally succeeds in 'rising' and in escaping from Middlemarch. Yet in her snobbish frustration, Rosamond inadvertently expresses a more profound unease with the Middlemarch environment. It is an unease that is magnified in the situations of Bulstrode and Farebrother. These two characters, like Rosamond, welcome Lydgate's arrival. Bulstrode 'certainly liked him the better, as Rosamond did, for being a stranger in Middlemarch. One can begin so many things with a new person! – even begin to be a better man' (p. 153). And Farebrother says to Lydgate, '"I can't spare you. You are a sort of circumnavigator come to settle among us, and will keep up my belief in the antipodes. Now tell me all about them in Paris"' (p. 206). The contentment and security of Middlemarch life can obviously be stifling and tedious to some.

A central affirmation of the value of life within the community exists in the portrayal of the Garths, with their loyalty, tolerance and rootedness, and in the commitment of Fred and Mary to each other. This area of the novel tends to show a benevolent liking for some aspects of provincialism. It may be that such a picture of contentment is nostalgia on the part of George Eliot for the lost way of life in her childhood, before religious doubt and intellectual curiosity crossed her path.

On the other hand, the portrayal of rumour and prejudice is essentially hostile in tone, sympathy being given to those who suffer in Middlemarch. The treatment of Rosamond, the perfect provincial young lady, contributes to this condemnation by demonstrating the rigidity and pettiness of her brand of gentility. An interesting episode is the faintly comic interview between Mrs Bulstrode and Rosamond, which serves to precipitate Rosamond's engagement. As the women sit down together, they automatically assess and note each other's expensive clothing, weighing up the claims of age, money, and social status. Mrs Bulstrode questions Rosamond, who declares that she is not engaged:

'How is it that every one says so, then – that it is the town's talk?'

'The town's talk is of very little consequence, I think,' said Rosamond, inwardly gratified.

'Oh, my dear, be more thoughtful; don't despise your neighbours so.' (p. 330)

The town's talk is simultaneously something to deplore as vulgar, something to fear, and something to be gratified to figure in. Rosamond despises it, but in fact it aids her in her becoming engaged to Lydgate, and the weight of familial and social ties supports her in her troubles with Lydgate. Much later, it is to be the greatest fear propelling her to thwart him in his plans for retrenchment. Mrs Bulstrode does not purvey gossip, but makes intelligent use of it here. Later she, and Rosamond, are to become its victims:

There were hardly any wives in Middlemarch whose matrimonial misfortunes would in different ways be likely to call forth more of this moral activity than Rosamond and her aunt Bulstrode. (p. 798)

The power of rumour, opinion and gossip is a major element in *Middlemarch*, in part because it constitutes those evolutionary 'conditions' or environment that work upon the individual organism. The blind workings of conditions become here the atmosphere of ignorance, which promotes rumour, which in turn promotes prejudice. Lydgate is perhaps aware of the irony of his explanation when he tells Mrs Bulstrode that her husband is ill because '"There is often something poisonous in the air of public rooms"' (p. 803). That poison, prejudice, often causes a kind of martyrdom for those who are misunderstood.

The Prelude signals that the novel is to concern itself with martyrdom, and while Dorothea's willingness to become a martyr is treated somewhat ironically at first, a genuine martyrdom awaits both her and Lydgate. Chapters 44 and 45 are about the problems that Lydgate experiences when Bulstrode is attempting to institute the new Fever Hospital with Lydgate in charge. The section begins with Lydgate enlisting Dorothea's moral (and financial) support for the venture. Dorothea interprets his efforts in the light of her own aspirations, envying him: '"How happy you must be, to know things that you feel sure will do great good!"' (p. 479). She applauds the grandiose aims of bringing improved medical facilities to Middlemarch, and of reforming medicine, and amusingly exaggerates to herself the difficulties experienced by Lydgate and Bulstrode, 'looking at the affairs of Middlemarch by the light of the great persecutions' (p. 478). Yet the authorial irony in this description of Dorothea's reaction quickly disappears. A catalogue of Lydgate's efforts to introduce change, and of the ways in which the general community resists him, underlines the huge difficulties that Lydgate is facing. He has wanted to learn more by means of dissection, and has offended the community by proposing to dissect a venerable old lady who has died. He has tried 'the expectant theory ... watching the course of an interesting disease when left as much as possible to itself, so that the stages might be noted for future guidance' (pp. 490–1) on Borthrop Trumbull with more success. But his general aims and ambitions are misunderstood, feared, and translated into defects of his character, by patients and fellow doctors alike. He is disliked for his apparent arrogance, and even imputed with charlatanism behind his back. The struggle between reformer and community is focused in the epigraph to Chapter 45, which quotes Sir Thomas Browne's ironic description of conservatism: 'condemning the vices of their own times, by the expressions of vices in times which they commend, which cannot but argue the community of vice in both' (p. 481). Lydgate is encountering those who propagate 'the community of vice'. He comforts himself by recalling Vesalius, and George Eliot explicitly invites the reader to contemplate martyrdom:

Many thoughts cheered him at that time – and justly. A man conscious of enthusiasm for worthy aims is sustained under petty hostilities by the memory of great workers who had to fight their way not without wounds, and who hover in his mind as patron saints, invisibly helping. (p. 496)

Lydgate is to become a martyr in more than one way. The episode of the new Fever Hospital also indicates the continual struggle of all the reformers in the novel, and the way that Middlemarch consistently reacts to events in a wider national arena. In *George Eliot and Community*, Suzanne Graver remarks,

The resistance of traditional community to change and the need to break free from provincial boundaries – from hereditary custom, habitual practice, and inherited institutions – are suggested all the way through the novel, in part by locating the desire for reform in characters who are outsiders.

The associative cluster, in *Middlemarch*, of reformers, outsiders and national politics that Graver points out here is most evident in the figure of Ladislaw, when he becomes editor of Brooke's newly acquired newspaper, *The Pioneer*, and develops an increasing commitment to politics through his journalism. Brooke's patronage may appear to assimilate Ladislaw into Middlemarch, but in fact, rather than accepting Ladislaw, Middlemarch rejects Brooke. However, history is on Ladislaw's side, it seems. In Chapters 37 and 38, the news that Brooke has bought *The Pioneer* is discussed at length. Ladislaw comes in for some scathing criticism behind his back. Sir James expostulates, '"There are stories going about him as a quill-driving alien, a foreign emissary, and what not ... it's a disagreeable affair all round. What a character for anybody with decent connections to show himself in! – one of those newspaper fellows!"' (pp. 414, 415). Sir James is expressing a contempt for newspaper men which was prevalent in the 1830s, when they were suspected of radicalism and sedition. Alan J. Lee quotes *The London Review* in 1835:

the Newspaper Press is thus degraded from the rank of a liberal profession: the employment and the class engaged in it sink: and the conduct of our journals falls too much into the hands of men of obscure birth, imperfect education, blunt feelings and coarse manners, who are accustomed to a low position in society, and are contented to be excluded from a circle in which they have never been used to move.[2]

The general attitude towards Ladislaw in Middlemarch coincides with a general refusal of Middlemarchers to recognize that national concern over Reform has anything to do with them. Yet while at first the rival papers in Middlemarch, *The Pioneer* and *The Trumpet*, confuse their readers, they serve to educate opinion. Ladislaw contributes to this education, for he '"can write the highest style of leading article, quite equal to anything in the London papers"' (p. 393), and from this point in the novel, there is increased discussion of political issues. In Chapter 46, we are told that 'there was a new political animation in Middlemarch' (p. 499).

Ladislaw's optimism seems to carry him towards being a successful public man despite the numerous calumnies voiced behind his back. This is particularly shown in an exchange between him and Lydgate, where he maintains an optimistic view of the usefulness of working for Reform, while Lydgate discounts such vague action. In the following passage, it is Lydgate who is speaking first:

'You go against rottenness, and there is nothing more thoroughly rotten than making people believe that society can be cured by a political hocus-pocus.'
    'That's very fine, my dear fellow. But your cure must begin somewhere, and put it that a thousand things which debase a population can never be reformed without this particular reform to begin with.' (p. 506)

Lydgate is martyred because of the force of public opinion. Brooke's ordeal at the hustings also shows the humiliation of being subject to crowds. Yet Ladislaw is ultimately not a victim but an originator of opinion. Alan J. Lee tells us that in the mid-nineteenth century, 'information, guidance and the erosion of parochialism ... were considered to be the first tasks of the newspaper press',[3] and Ladislaw is therefore prophetic when he dreams to himself, 'political writing, political speaking, would get a higher value now public life was going to be wider and more national' (p. 550). He is a man of the future in his identification with the press and with politics.

However, if there is an optimism, in the treatment of politics, that change will prevail, and that Middlemarch might even concede to such change, the coming of the railways poses a different confrontation between the provinces and the metropolis. In Chapter 56 Caleb Garth comes across some labourers of the Lowick parish fighting with men from the railway companies. At first it seems that Middlemarch is reacting with the usual ignorance, suspicion and resistance. Mr Solomon and Mrs Waule have voiced instinctive disapproval of anything strange and new, and Solomon has incited the labourers. Caleb Garth takes the view that '"It's all ignorance. Somebody has been telling them lies. The poor fools don't know any better"' (p. 603), and he says to them, '"It may do a bit of harm here and there, to this and to that; and so does the sun in heaven. But the railway's a good thing"' (p. 604). But his seemingly humane and pragmatic arguments are met with a denial that argues from another point of view:

'I'n seen lots o' things turn up sin' I war a young un – the war an' the peace, and the canells, an' the oald King George, an' the Regen', an' the new King George, an' the new un as has got a new ne-ame – an' it's been all aloike to the poor mon. What's the canells been t' him? They'n brought him neyther me-at nor be-acon, nor wage to lay by, if he didn't save it wi' clemmin' his own inside. Times ha' got wusser for him sin' I war a young un. An' so it'll be wi' the railroads. They'll on'y leave the poor mon furder behind.' (p. 604)

To some extent, this alternative point of view, which justifies conservatism when reform is associated with capitalist growth, is undercut by George Eliot's use of dialect. Timothy Cooper, the speaker here, is relegated to the status of rustic chorus, because he does not share the language of any of the main characters in the novel – he is marginalized within the language of the novel. Yet the voicing of an alternative point of view remains as a presence, even despite the urbane, and therefore equally dismissive, description of Caleb Garth's difficulties:

Caleb was in a difficulty known to any person attempting in dark times and unassisted by miracle to reason with rustics who are in possession of an undeniable truth which they know through a hard process of feeling, and can let it fall like a giant's club on your neatly-carved argument for a social benefit which they do *not* feel. (p. 605)

In the section 'The Multiplot Novel', I commented on the paradoxical way in which the structure of the novel conveys both unity and diversity. In its title, *Middlemarch* confirms the notion of an organic community. Yet alongside images of contentment and security, there exist powerful examples of dissent and division. There is constant difference among members of the community, and resistance to elements from outside that introduce the 'new'. At times the community expels those individuals who will not fit in; at other times it appears to be about to adapt. But in general, there is a frightening coercion of public identity at the expense of some of the characters, only partly mitigated by George Eliot's concern for social duty, family and environment.

2. Themes

For George Eliot, as for many thoughtful Victorians, the existence of human egoism – be it called selfishness, subjectivity or self-consciousness – was perplexing to contemplate. In the light of evolutionary theories, egoism represented a self-seeking core of human nature, linking human beings to the animal and plant worlds. The philosophies of Feuerbach, Spinoza and Comte offered some solutions, as we have seen, in their various advocacies of human striving towards sympathy and altruism. An examination of egoism, and a persuasive enthusiasm for a development from egoism to altruism, are striking to any reader of *Middlemarch*. This powerful theme is in effect the basic ideology that informs the novel, although George Eliot is not unaware of the complexities involved.

A helpful place to begin is with the famous passage in Chapter 27, where the narrator provides a metaphor that compels the reader to concur with a view that human beings inevitably read all events as pertaining to themselves and their own interests:

Your pier-glass or extensive surface of polished steel made to be rubbed by a housemaid, will be minutely and multitudinously scratched in all directions; but place now against it a lighted candle as a centre of illumination, and lo! the scratches will seem to arrange themselves in a fine series of concentric circles round that little sun. It is demonstrable that the scratches are going everywhere impartially, and it is only your candle which produces the flattering illusion of a concentric arrangement, its light falling with an exclusive optical selection. These things are a parable. The scratches are events, and the candle is the egoism of any person now absent . . . (p. 297)

The passage goes on to discuss Rosamond, yet the observation of the effect of a single source of light on a reflective surface presses towards a general truth, because it carries the authority of objectivity. This claim for the 'truth' of human egoism should be read alongside the equally compelling statement in the final line of the epigraph to Chapter 81. This is the point at which Dorothea – and Rosamond, to some extent – rises above her own desires and emotions. The line comes from Goethe's *Faust*: 'Zum höchsten Dasein immerfort zu streben' (849). It may be translated as 'Eternally to strive towards the highest state of being'. Here, the authority of another text, *Faust*, is brought into play to underline George Eliot's philosophy.

To George Eliot, then, human beings are inevitably but not unchangeably egoists. In its universality, this human 'weakness' calls out her sympathy, a sympathy which many of the characters must strive towards. The authorial voice also frequently addresses the reader directly, thereby implicating him or her in the characters' foibles: the reader must identify her or himself with human egoism, and must extend sympathy to the characters. For example, Bulstrode's cast of mind and reliance on Providence are essentially products of his egoism. The narrator points this out and refuses to condemn what is, after all, a common human failing:

There may be coarse hypocrites, who consciously affect beliefs and emotions for the sake of gulling the world, but Bulstrode was not one of them. He was simply a man whose desires had been stronger than his theoretic beliefs, and who had gradually explained the gratification of his desires into satisfactory agreement with those beliefs. If this be hypocrisy, it is a process which shows itself occasionally in us all, to whatever confession we belong . . . (p. 667)

Similarly, Casaubon, trapped in a 'prison' of egoism, is presented to the reader in Chapter 29 as having a claim on the reader's attention equal to that of any younger character, for 'Mr Casaubon had an intense consciousness within him, and was spiritually a-hungered like the rest of us' (p. 312). This emphasis on 'us' – the commonness of human experience – and on the need for compassion has been expressed earlier when the narrator says:

Mr Casaubon, too, was the centre of his own world; if he was liable to think that others were providentially made for him . . . this trait is not quite alien to us, and, like the other mendicant hopes of mortals, claims some of our pity. (p. 111)

In all these instances, there is considerable pressure on the reader to concur with the author's analysis of human nature.

According to this version of experience, egoism is a lowly state, from which the individual must strive to rise. The tone of sympathy for egoists actually at times implies distance, for it is matched in the text by moral approval for those who escape their own concerns: Dorothea, pre-eminently, but also Lydgate, Ladislaw, Fred, Mrs Bulstrode and Farebrother. Development from egoism to sympathy and altruism, while a development of progress and improvement, involves suffering as the individual learns that what she or he wishes cannot always prevail. There is, indeed, eternal conflict between the universal egoism of individuals and the necessity for social duty. That the individual must learn through suffering is, in *Middlemarch*, unavoidable, and this helps to give the novel its innately sombre tone.

The narrator shows how external circumstances in varying guises impinge upon the individual, forcing him or her to relinquish personal desires. Mrs Bulstrode, for example, must renounce her pleasures in status and finery to support her erring, and grieving, husband; Fred must face the reality of his lack of money and occupation and try to succeed in a different sphere; Mr Farebrother must stand back from his love for Mary, and is asked by Fred to promote *his* suit. Lydgate must recognize and accept the limitations of his life, and Ladislaw spends a great part of the novel trying to come to terms with what seems a hopeless devotion to Dorothea.

In all these examples, though, it is evident that the reasons for suffering differ, and consequently the degree of personal responsibility and the degree of moral stature differ. In each case there is a mixture of a compulsion to act in one way rather than another, and a decision to act. Mrs Bulstrode is forced to respond to changing circumstances, but unlike Rosamond, she moves towards her husband in sympathy; Fare-brother is asked by Fred to intercede with Mary, but he chooses freely not to compete; Fred cannot avoid the seeming injustice of Feather-stone's will, and must reconsider his future, but he works hard. The many and complex influences bearing on Lydgate have already been discussed. Ladislaw, perhaps, never fully demonstrates a resignation to circumstance or a resolution to act.

The individual, then, while wedded to his or her own subjectivity, is forced to respond to the experiences of living alongside other people, of being a member of a human society, and of being affected by external events and circumstance. This theme leads the way to intensive psychological portrayal. It produces a vision of existence that verges on the deterministic. It also provides the opportunity for an examination of profound conflict, as individuals inevitably clash in their interests. And it poses the question of legitimate claims for and against the self: the renunciation of self can sometimes be the annihilation of self, as others' priorities take precedence.

Casaubon enters the novel when he meets Dorothea and swiftly becomes her (less than ardent) suitor. Isolation and the life of a scholar have enabled him to live apart from other people for the majority of his life. He cannot reach out to others or respond to them, and he fears criticism and even pity. His constant presence in the library symbolizes his imprisonment and his retreat into egoism from the suspected sneers of others. His injunction that he is not to be disturbed there, and his reluctance to allow Dorothea to join him, show the self-imposed suffering of extreme egoism. Casaubon's story is in part the painful process whereby he must learn to live with another human being. But partly because he is continually associated with solitude and death, and partly because he is to become the means of Dorothea's fuller growth out of egoism, he does not demonstrate as a character that development from egoism to altruism in any great depth. It is his selfishness, first in proposing that Dorothea continue his labour after his death, and then in modifying his will, that propels the story of Dorothea, and our remaining impression of him is negative. Yet while he is a living presence in the novel, he is treated by the author with considerable sympathy. Not only does he represent a pathetic but intense scholarship, but he also faces the ultimate solitude of mortality. His illness and awareness of approaching death are the fullest expression in the novel of the question of individual extinction and the selfish but natural desire to remain a presence in the world, shown also in Featherstone and Raffles. In Chapter 42, Lydgate tells Casaubon, at his request, the prognosis of his condition, and Casaubon must face the reality of his own death for the first time. The situation is movingly described:

the black figure with hands behind and head bent forward continued to pace the walk where the dark yew-trees gave him a mute companionship in melancholy, and the little shadows of bird or leaf that fleeted across the isles of sunlight, stole along in silence as in the presence of a sorrow. Here was a man who now for the first time found himself looking into the eyes of death ... To Mr Casaubon now, it was as if he suddenly found himself on the dark river-brink and heard the plash of the oncoming oar, not discerning the forms, but expecting the summons. (pp. 461, 462)

The vocabulary here provides numerous signs of death and solitude: 'black', 'dark yew-trees', 'mute', 'melancholy', 'shadows', for example. It is at this point that Dorothea's painful experiences of marriage to Casaubon collide with his introversion. She has already found that she is living a 'nightmare of a life in which every energy was arrested by dread' (p. 410). She timidly goes out to offer him company and comfort, but when she puts her hand through his arm, he 'kept his hands behind him and allowed her pliant arm to cling with difficulty against his rigid arm' (p. 462). This rejection reduces Dorothea to a state of bitter criticism: 'In the jar of her whole being, Pity was overthrown. Was it her fault that she had believed in him – had believed in his worthiness?' (pp. 463–4). There is no simple answer to who is right or wrong, good or bad, here. The irreconcilable claims of individual experience seem to prevail: Casaubon is facing the loneliest and most chilling moment of his life, but is shunning companionship; Dorothea is suffering rejection and disappointment, but is giving way to temper. Out of this conflict comes a temporary reconciliation, though, and perhaps it is significant that the end of this chapter is the end of the fourth Book of *Middlemarch*: structurally, the moment comes at exactly the mid-point of the novel. In the course of a solitary evening, Dorothea achieves some self-control and sympathy (and that it is her point of view that is given here tilts our sympathy towards her, away from Casaubon):

That thought with which Dorothea had gone out to meet her husband – her conviction that he had been asking about the possible arrest of all his work, and that the answer must have wrung his heart, could not be long without rising beside the image of him, like a shadowy monitor looking at her anger with sad remonstrance. It cost her a litany of pictured sorrows and of silent cries that she might be the mercy for those sorrows – but the resolved submission did come; (p. 464)

She waits on the landing for when Casaubon might leave the library, and her timid generosity is rewarded by Casaubon's gentle greeting:

'Come, my dear, come. You are young, and need not to extend your life by watching.'
    When the kind quiet melancholy of that speech fell on Dorothea's ears, she felt something like the thankfulness that might well up in us if we had narrowly escaped hurting a lamed creature. She put her hand into her husband's, and they went along the broad corridor together. (p. 465)

Dorothea has succeeded in imaginatively living another's experience, and thinks of Casaubon as 'a lamed creature'. Casaubon, like Dorothea, and possibly in response to her generosity of spirit, for a time transcends his selfish concerns. Thus the first half of the novel ends on a note of selflessness and companionship, as Dorothea and Casaubon walk 'along the broad corridor', a common metaphor for the idea of moving into the future, hand in hand.

Dorothea's progress through the novel from a girlhood of ardent opinion and egoism to a womanhood of sympathy and altruism is in many ways the model of George Eliot's analysis of egoism and its renunciation. Her marriage to Casaubon subjects her to many tests of her patience and pity. She learns to 'serve', not in the way that she confidently expected, but in a far less attractive manner: 'Dorothea had thought that she could have been patient with John Milton, but she had never imagined him behaving in this way; and for a moment Mr Casaubon seemed to be stupidly undiscerning and odiously unjust' (p. 316). This is on an early occasion when he assumes that she will wish for Ladislaw's visit against his own desires. Dorothea achieves what some readers feel to be a rather saccharine status as a 'good' woman, bearing the author's approbation for her forbearance, her efforts to see others' points of view, and her spreading of good will.

Yet in defence of this undeniably partisan narrative attitude, it should be noted that there are many intimations that too much self-denial can be dangerous, and even annihilating. The individual cannot exist without an ego, after all. Casaubon's selfishness must be at times resisted, as well as understood, by Dorothea. Later, Celia and Sir James, in their well-meaning but selfish claims, must be withstood. As Dorothea learns to quell her desires, she is in peril of losing direction and autonomy, and this is not aided by her position of leisured gentlewoman, with no duties or mission. She only just escapes making a binding promise to Casaubon before his death. With Lydgate's help, she returns to Lowick alone when she has become a widow, and with his help again, she appoints Farebrother to the Lowick living instead of Tyke, whom her uncle is recommending in a partisan spirit. This continuing ability to assert herself emerges as imperative in the ideology of the novel: it is Dorothea who finally breaks the silence with Will and tells him that she wants to marry him. However, the complexity of the treatment of egoism in the novel is evident even here, for we should also observe that this moment of Dorothea's 'will' has sprung from an equally charged moment of self-denial, when she has gone to speak to Rosamond against her innermost feelings.

Dorothea's education, and her status in the novel as a model of human striving and altruism, are not significant merely because of her improvement as an individual. George Eliot held the view that social harmony would spread through the influence of such selfless people. And so Dorothea is seen increasingly to have an important effect on others through example. At first, perhaps, she is shown to be quixotic and headstrong in her enthusiasms. Later, her difference from other people is cast as being threatening and odd:

Mrs Cadwallader said, privately, 'You will certainly go mad in that house alone, my dear. You will see visions. We have all got to exert ourselves a little to keep sane, and call things by the same name as other people call them by . . .'

'I never called everything by the same name that all the people about me did,' said Dorothea stoutly. (p. 581)

Eventually, however, she becomes an influential presence in the minds of Ladislaw, Lydgate and Rosamond. George Eliot shows through Dorothea's dominion the harmonious power of selflessness, and also the necessity for some individuals to hold fast to their personal view of the nature of things. With Ladislaw, for instance, Dorothea shows the way of sympathetic understanding, persuading him by example to be pitying of Casaubon:

'Perhaps,' she continued, getting into a pleading tone, 'my uncle has not told you how serious Mr Casaubon's illness was. It would be petty of us who are well and can bear things, to think much of small offences from those who carry a weight of trial.'

'You teach me better,' said Will. 'I will never grumble on that subject again.' (p. 402)

Lydgate can never forget her impulse of sympathy and devotion towards her husband, and it spurs him to be gentle with Rosamond:

His mind glancing back to Laure while he looked at Rosamond, he said inwardly, 'Would *she* kill me because I wearied her?' and then, 'It is the way with all women.' But this power of generalizing which gives men so much the superiority in mistake over the dumb animals, was immediately thwarted by Lydgate's memory of wondering impressions from the behaviour of another woman – from Dorothea's looks and tones of emotion about her husband when Lydgate began to attend him ... That voice of deep-souled womanhood had remained within him as the enkindling conceptions of dead and sceptred genius had remained within him (is there not a genius for feeling nobly which also reigns over human spirits and their conclusions?) (p. 638)

Dorothea's subtle power of influence for a 'growing good' is a major element in the theme of egoism. On a single occasion, in Chapter 81, she compels Rosamond to a similar display of altruism, although readers are divided on whether Rosamond merely mimics Dorothea, or whether she genuinely experiences an enlargement of her limited affections.

Rosamond is perhaps the most extreme example of egoism in the novel. From the very beginning, when she firmly believes that Lydgate is intended by Providence to be her husband, and sees Fred's illness as a mere device to bring her and Lydgate into proximity, her egoism is rampant. There are delightfully ironic points of characterization, such as when she contradicts Mary's comments on her plainness by the side of Rosamond:

'Oh no! No one thinks of your appearance, you are so sensible and useful, Mary. Beauty is of very little consequence in reality,' said Rosamond, turning her head towards Mary, but with eyes swerving towards the new view of her neck in the glass. (p. 140)

To look in a mirror is to regard one's self, in preference to looking outwards at others. And Rosamond's vain beauty, often detailed by a reference to her pretty neck, becomes a weapon in her resistance to Lydgate throughout their marital problems: when Lydgate first broaches their financial affairs, she 'turned her neck and looked at a vase on the mantelpiece' (p. 639). Through the catalogue of her passive and active resistance to Lydgate's wishes, she maintains her view of her own rightness and of the wrongness of anyone who contradicts her view of the world; she thinks bitterly of

disagreeable people who only thought of themselves, and did not mind how annoying they were to her. Even her father was unkind, and might have done more for them. In fact there was but one person in Rosamond's world whom she did not regard as blameworthy, and that was the graceful creature with blond plaits and with little hands crossed before her, who had never expressed herself unbecomingly, and had always acted for the best – the best naturally being what she best liked. (p. 716)

In this passage lies the basic irony of egoism: others are disagreeable for thinking 'only of themselves', but not the subject who is also thinking only of him or herself.

The association of egoism with animal instincts is subtly underlined in the portrayal of Rosamond. The conflicts between her and Lydgate are often expressed in images from biology, geology or zoology, and this is meant to show that Rosamond, and Lydgate to some extent – indeed, any egoist at full stretch – is in thrall to instinct. When Rosamond maintains that her riding was not the cause of the loss of her baby, Lydgate 'secretly wondered over the terrible tenacity of this mild creature' (p. 631). When she refuses to help him choose articles to return to Dover, 'It seemed that she had no more identified herself with him than if they had been creatures of different species and opposing interests' (pp. 642–3). Lydgate's experience of his growing problems makes him 'conscious of new elements in his life as noxious to him as an inlet of mud to a creature that has been used to breathe and bathe and dart after its illuminated prey in the clearest of waters' (p. 631). The evolutionary scenario of struggle and survival reaches its clearest expression when it becomes evident that Rosamond has a stronger will than Lydgate: 'As to saying that he was master, it was not the fact. The very resolution to which he had wrought himself by dint of logic and honourable pride was beginning to relax under her torpedo contact'

(p. 711). 'Torpedo' in this context refers to the fish, sometimes also known as cramp-fish or electric ray, which emits electric discharges. Lydgate is 'benumbed' when talking to Farebrother (p. 712): the result of having been stung by Rosamond.

The epigraph to Chapter 37 is a sonnet by Spenser, praising female constancy and steadfast purpose. Such a woman is 'like a steddy ship' keeping 'her course aright', and the final couplet states:

> Most happy she that most assured doth rest,
> But he most happy who such one loves best.
>
> (p. 392)

This chapter shows Dorothea talking to Ladislaw about Casaubon and to Casaubon about Ladislaw, and is the occasion when she suggests to Casaubon that his nephew has a genuine claim on his property, thus infuriating Casaubon unwittingly. We are told:

She was blind, you see, to many things obvious to others – likely to tread in the wrong places, as Celia had warned her; yet her blindness to whatever did not lie in her own pure purpose carried her safely by the side of precipices where vision would have been perilous with fear. (p. 408)

The reader admires Dorothea's 'own pure purpose' and observes the irony of Casaubon's response: instead of being 'he most happy who such one loves best', he suspects betrayal and manipulation. In a total contrast, the epigraph also has some relevance to the immediately preceding chapter, in which Rosamond prevails upon her father to allow her marriage to Lydgate to proceed. We are told that 'the circumstance called Rosamond was particularly forcible by means of that mild persistence which, as we know, enables a white soft living substance to make its way in spite of opposing rock' (p. 379). To Lydgate, her determination is 'adorable' (p. 385) – at this point he is that man 'most happy who such one loves best'. But Rosamond's strength of will is extreme egoism, while Dorothea's is 'pure' and selfless. This can be seen in the contrast between Rosamond's statement, '"I never give up anything that I choose to do"' (p. 385) and the exchange,

'I was very fond of doing as I liked, but I have almost given it up,' [Dorothea] ended, smiling playfully.

'I have not given up doing as I like, but I can very seldom do it,' said Will. (p. 589)

Fittingly, Rosamond's come-uppance is delivered through someone else – Ladislaw – who is thinking very much of himself and not of her feelings. The extremity of the destruction of her ego is in proportion to the monstrous exercise of her own desires and will hitherto. After Dorothea has inadvertently disturbed Rosamond and Ladislaw together, he cannot refrain from expressing his frustration. Rosamond at first resorts to her usual frigid behaviour: 'In flute-like tones of sarcasm she said, "You can easily go after Mrs Casaubon and explain your preference"' (p. 835), but such genteel vocabulary is only a weapon handed to Ladislaw in his turmoil:

'Explain! Tell a man to explain how he dropped into hell! Explain my preference! I never had a *preference* for her, any more than I have a preference for breathing. No other woman exists by the side of her. I would rather touch her hand if it were dead, than I would touch any other woman's living.' (pp. 835–6)

Rosamond, having existed solely within her own ego, temperament, desires and feelings, is almost entirely obliterated. She 'was almost losing the sense of her identity, and seemed to be waking into some new terrible existence'; 'What another nature felt in opposition to her own was being burnt and bitten into her consciousness'; 'her little world was in ruins, and she felt herself tottering in the midst as a lonely bewildered consciousness' (pp. 836, 837).

Even while Rosamond is receiving some kind of come-uppance, though, she becomes the pitiful victim of another's egoism. The description of her 'mute misery' (p. 837) tends to turn the reader's reaction to one of compassion, and this is further encouraged by the authorial comments attempting to excuse Ladislaw's cruelty (thereby drawing attention to that same cruelty): 'Let it be forgiven to Will that he had no such movement of pity' (p. 836).

When Dorothea and Rosamond meet in Chapter 81, both have, by varying routes, reached a point of self-denial: Dorothea through long and hard experience, Rosamond at the hands of Ladislaw. Both are ready to give and sympathize, rather than to assert their own emotions at the expense of the other. Dorothea attempts to explain Lydgate to his wife; Rosamond attempts to explain Ladislaw to Dorothea. Yet it would not be just to equate Dorothea's struggle to gain perception with Rosamond's recent shock. There is a sense in which Rosamond is in a mood to be swayed by Dorothea, and Dorothea is stronger than Lydgate to do so. Rosamond 'felt something like bashful timidity before a superior, in the presence of this self-forgetful ardour' (p. 853). She is 'taken hold of by an emotion stronger than her own' (p. 856), and tells Dorothea that Ladislaw loves her more than he could love herself. But even at this point, we are told: 'She had begun her confession under the subduing influence of Dorothea's emotion; and as she went on she had gathered the sense that she was repelling Will's reproaches, which were still like a knife-wound within her' (p. 856). Rosamond is reverting to an egoistic reason for what she does and says. However, it is also important to note that egoism may in this instance be a valiant effort at self-preservation, for Rosamond has very nearly been annihilated.

Another major theme in *Middlemarch* is marriage. The novel eschews the conventional plot of courtship leading to matrimony in the closing pages, and concentrates on what happens after two people have married each other. On the whole, marriages in *Middlemarch* are unhappy. The exceptions – Celia and Sir James, Fred and Mary – form a background of conventional marital happiness and conventional plot development. In the foreground, we witness the conflicts, disappointments and mis-understandings of two couples, Dorothea and Casaubon, and Lydgate and Rosamond. Marriage, as a social as well as a personal contract, becomes a metaphor for the integration of the individual into society, and is the personal relationship through which George Eliot portrays the inescapable threats to the ego that living with another human being causes. The prevailing tone of *Middlemarch* is irony: it is the reversal of expectation from courtship to the reality of marriage that figures promi-nently.

In his review of *Middlemarch*, Henry James commented:

Each is a tale of matrimonial infelicity, but the conditions in each are so different and the circumstances so broadly opposed that the mind passes from one to the other with that supreme sense of the vastness and variety of human life, under aspects apparently similar, which it belongs only to the greatest novels to produce.

Despite James's perception of variety and difference, though, there are some general points of similarity. George Eliot seems to demonstrate that the sexes enter marriage with quite differing and even unreasonable expectations. For example, both Casaubon and Lydgate find courtship a time-consuming and preoccupying period which takes them away from their researches, and both look forward to being married, when they shall be able, they think, to resume the 'real' business of their lives. Meanwhile, Dorothea and Rosamond, in different ways, both confi-dently expect to become the central figure in their husbands' lives. Marriage means quite opposing things to men and to women.

Beyond this observation of a tragic gulf between the sexes, there is little to link the two stories. Casaubon marries because 'he had always intended to acquit himself by marriage' (p. 312) and he is growing older. Even before marrying, he has discovered that it has been over-rated: 'the poets had much exaggerated the force of masculine passion' (p. 87); in fact, as Celia says, '"I think he is not half fond enough of Dorothea"' (pp. 318–9). He discovers that in marrying Dorothea he has invited into his closest world a critic just like all the critics he fears and avoids. He has sought a secretary, yet he cannot bear Dorothea's help. He cannot abandon his own egoism and recognize the individuality of the person he has married.

Dorothea's experience of marriage is in almost every way a reversal of the expectations she had treasured as a girl. The most interesting passage is that in which her horrified reactions to Rome coalesce with, and form an objective correlative to, her realization of what her marriage is to be. We are told of

the dream-like strangeness of her bridal life. Dorothea had now been five weeks in Rome, and in the kindly mornings when autumn and winter seemed to go hand in hand like a happy aged couple one of whom would presently survive in chiller loneliness, she had driven about at first with Mr Casaubon, but of late chiefly with Tantripp and their experienced courier. (p. 224)

The simile of the 'happy aged couple' works to underline the lack of such companionship between Dorothea and her husband, but it also conveys the inappropriateness of Dorothea's solitary trips during a honeymoon: an elderly couple may well expect future solitude, but a newly married couple should look forward to being together. The passage continues by stressing the distressed and hallucinatory state of mind of Dorothea – 'oppressive masquerade', 'enigmatical', 'un-intelligible', and this mounts to a description of the physical forms that she is forced to contemplate:

the dimmer but yet eager Titanic life gazing and struggling on walls and ceilings; the long vistas of white forms whose marble eyes seemed to hold the monotonous light of an alien world: all this vast wreck of ambitious ideals, sensuous and spiritual, mixed confusedly with the signs of breathing forgetfulness and degrada-tion, at first jarred her as with an electric shock, and then urged themselves on her with that ache belonging to a glut of confused ideas which check the flow of emotion. Forms both pale and glowing took possession of her young sense, and fixed themselves in her memory even when she was not thinking of them, preparing strange associations which remained through her after-years. (p. 225)

The intricacy and force of this passage may well confuse the reader unless it is read as information about Dorothea's response to sexuality and to an energy that her husband certainly does not possess. Dorothea is disturbed and unwillingly affected by the sense of movement and sensual life that she contemplates: the words, 'electric shock' and 'ache', convey her reluctant response. In contrast, her dismay at the history of Rome, a 'vast wreck of ambitious ideals', symbolizes both her revulsion from the aged man she has married and the wreck of her own aspirations.

The very forcefulness of this passage intimates how significant it is as a message concerning Dorothea's married life. Her education through marriage to Casaubon is discussed elsewhere. The estrangement of the couple is shown in the final hours of Casaubon's life, when he attempts to wrest from her a promise to continue his work, and Dorothea must resist:

'You refuse?' said Mr Casaubon, with more edge in his tone.

'No, I do not yet refuse,' said Dorothea, in a clear voice, the need of freedom asserting itself within her; 'but it is too solemn – I think it is not right – to make a promise when I am ignorant what it will bind me to. Whatever affection prompted I would do without promising.' (p. 519)

Casaubon's work strikes Dorothea now as 'a theory which was already withered in the birth like an elfin child' (p. 519). The marriage has been equally sterile and fruitless. When Casaubon dies, he dies alone, and at a time when Dorothea is reluctant even to go to him as he awaits her in the garden. On her return to Lowick as a widow, her mute and futile message to Casaubon conveys the history of their marriage, in which she has been reaching out to communicate with him while he has been retreating into his comforting prison of solitude: '"I could not use it. Do you not see now that I could not submit my soul to yours, by working hopelessly at what I have no belief in? – Dorothea"' (p. 583).

In his Introduction to the Penguin edition of *Middlemarch*, W. J. Harvey comments on how 'this so abruptly concluded relationship is extended in the novel by Lydgate's parallel attitude to Rosamond; the theme is, so to speak, unconsciously passed from one character to another' (p. 12). The relationship between Lydgate and Rosamond is a mixture of desire, reluctance and unsuitability. Rosamond identifies Lydgate as a prospective husband even before they have met, because of his difference from Middlemarch men, his social rank, and his profession. She is more than ready to fall in love with him, and that is what she thinks she does:

He reached the whip before she did, and turned to present it to her. She bowed and looked at him: he of course was looking at her, and their eyes met with that peculiar meeting which is never arrived at by effort, but seems like a sudden divine clearance of haze. I think Lydgate turned a little paler than usual, but Rosamond blushed deeply and felt a certain astonishment ... Yet this result, which she took to be a mutual impression, called falling in love, was just what Rosamond had contemplated beforehand. (p. 145)

Rosamond thinks of marriage in terms of 'the costume and introductions of her wedded life, having determined on her house in Middlemarch' (p. 146). When she finds that she is expected to relinquish precisely those acquisitions of marriage – jewels, furniture, house – Lydgate thinks bitterly: 'After all, . . . what can a woman care about so much as house and furniture? a husband without them is an absurdity' (p. 706).

Lydgate, on the other hand, has equally fixed, but different, preconceptions about marriage. In revulsion from the dramatic intensity of Laure, he imagines 'reclining in a paradise with sweet laughs for bird-notes, and blue eyes for a heaven' (p. 122). He expects a submissive and uninquiring admiration for his work, and assumes the superiority of men over women. Ironically, on one of the occasions when he enjoys such a tranquil paradise, it is broken by Rosamond's assertion of her will:

Rosamond played the quiet music which was as helpful to his meditation as the plash of an oar on the evening lake. It was rather late; he had pushed away all the books, and was looking at the fire with his hands clasped behind his head in forgetfulness of everything except the construction of a new controlling experiment, when Rosamond, who had left the piano and was leaning back in her chair watching him, said – 'Mr Ned Plymdale has taken a house already.' (p. 706)

Unlike Rosamond, Lydgate does not willingly fall in love. Their marriage is given a nudge forward by public opinion, in the form of Mrs Bulstrode's respectable inquiries, which causes Lydgate to retreat, and Rosamond to feel genuinely bereft; consequently, when they do meet again, both feel emotional. Lydgate is then overwhelmed by his innate tenderness towards those who are vulnerable:

as he raised his eyes now he saw a certain helpless quivering which touched him quite newly, and made him look at Rosamond with a questioning flash. At this moment she was as natural as she had ever been when she was five years old ... That moment of naturalness was the crystallizing feather-touch: it shook flirtation into love. (p. 335)

At this moment, Lydgate is profoundly affected by Rosamond's naturalness, but also by her femininity. And their engagement, a time of marvellous romance, also confirms that they live in separate worlds of illusion, far away from a realistic appraisal of each other.

George Eliot analyses the sources of their discontent in great detail, showing the reader the financial worries, the pressures of Lydgate's work, the loss of their child. But at the centre, there is a fundamental disappointment with each other. Lydgate finds that Rosamond cannot share his enthusiasm for his researches, while Rosamond finds marriage tedious after the homage and flirtation she had enjoyed as an unmarried girl. The struggle to maintain a love between them hardly succeeds. Rosamond becomes 'in such entire disgust with her husband that she wished that she had never seen him' (p. 716). Lydgate dimly realizes the potential failure:

His marriage would be a mere piece of bitter irony if they could not go on loving each other. He had long ago made up his mind to what he thought was her negative character – her want of sensibility, which showed itself in disregard both of his specific wishes and of his general aims. The first great disappointment had been borne: the tender devotedness and docile adoration of the ideal wife must be renounced, and life must be taken up on a lower stage of expectation, as it is by men who have lost their limbs. But the real wife had not only her claims, she had still a hold on his heart, and it was his intense desire that the hold should remain strong. In marriage, the certainty, 'She will never love me much', is easier to bear than the fear, 'I shall love her no more.' (p. 702)

Ultimately, the marriage subsides into a tired compromise with each other, and when Rosamond turns to Lydgate after her painful enlightenment at the hands of Ladislaw, Lydgate responds:

Poor Rosamond's vagrant fancy had come back terribly scourged – meek enough to nestle under the old despised shelter. And the shelter was still there: Lydgate had accepted his narrowed lot with sad resignation. He had chosen this fragile creature, and had taken the burthen of her life upon his arms. He must walk as he could, carrying that burthen pitifully. (p. 858)

This response resembles Dorothea's efforts towards compassion and acceptance in other situations. Indeed, Lydgate and Dorothea are linked together indirectly at the moment when Dorothea looks out of her window after a night of grief and struggle:

She opened her curtains, and looked out towards the bit of road that lay in view, with fields beyond, outside the entrance-gates. On the road there was a man with a bundle on his back and a woman carrying her baby; . . . She was a part of that involuntary, palpitating life, and could neither look out on it from her luxurious shelter as a mere spectator, nor hide her eyes in selfish complaining. (p. 846)

Lydgate might be the man carrying a bundle whom Dorothea sees. Both Dorothea and Lydgate take up their respective burdens after histories of struggle and disappointment. However, their stories are dissimilar as well as similar, and part of the reason for Lydgate's resignation – and even Rosamond's – is Dorothea's influence, which works upon both of them.

We have already seen how Lydgate perceives the prospective disaster of his marriage; Dorothea's tears in Rome express a similar dismay at the future with Casaubon. Many characters face an internal verdict of failure in the course of the novel, be it with regard to marriage, or work, or spiritual aspiration. When Bulstrode is asked in public either to deny the allegations being made against him, or to resign from public appointments, 'The quick vision that his life was after all a failure ... rushed through him like the agony of terror' (p. 781). Casaubon is beset with suspicions of the failure of his life's work. Perhaps the most moving instance is the information given in the Finale that Lydgate 'always regarded himself as a failure' (p. 893) despite the fact that he became a successful practitioner in London and on the continent.

The notions of failure and success permeate *Middlemarch*, and George Eliot takes a curiously oblique attitude towards them. On the one hand, she asks the reader to see Casaubon's case as tragic:

are there many situations more sublimely tragic than the struggle of the soul with the demand to renounce a work which has been all the significance of its life – a significance which is to vanish as the waters which come and go where no man has need of them? (p. 460)

This compassionate response corresponds to Dorothea's reaction:

She was no longer struggling against the perception of facts, but adjusting herself to their clearest perception; and now when she looked steadily at her husband's failure, still more at his possible consciousness of failure, she seemed to be looking along the one track where duty became tenderness. (p. 400)

On the other hand, Dorothea's earlier distress in Rome is treated with a mixture of dismissal and appeal for the reader's profound concern:

Nor can I suppose that when Mrs Casaubon is discovered in a fit of weeping six weeks after her wedding, the situation will be regarded as tragic. Some discouragement, some faintness of heart at the new real future which replaces the imaginary, is not unusual, and we do not expect people to be deeply moved by what is not unusual. That element of tragedy which lies in the very fact of frequency, has not yet wrought itself into the coarse emotion of mankind; and perhaps our frames could hardly bear much of it. (p. 226)

This commentary shifts from observing that 'discouragement . . . at the new real future' is a common reaction, to implying that just because something is common, that does not mean that it is not tragic. However, the commentary proceeds to suggest that such an encompassing apprehension of tragedy would be unbearable:

If we had a keen vision and feeling of all ordinary human life, it would be like hearing the grass grow and the squirrel's heart beat, and we should die of that roar which lies on the other side of silence. As it is, the quickest of us walk about well wadded with stupidity. (p. 226)

These memorable similes seem to suggest that a constant recognition of the tragedy in many lives would be too sombre to live with, and that 'stupidity' is a prerequisite for survival. This is one of several points in the novel where contradictions overwhelm the ideological clarity of the text. George Eliot is simultaneously pointing the reader towards sympathy with failure, and admitting that so pervasive does that failure appear, it is better not to dwell on it.

Failure in a less absolute and intense form also finds its way into the theme of work. Gillian Beer suggests that *Middlemarch* 'is about work and the right to work, about the need to discover a vocation which will satisfy the whole self and to be educated to undertake it'. Dorothea's question, 'What could she do, what ought she to do?' (p. 50) is, as we have seen, echoed by other characters. Many cannot find an answer; others do not fulfil what they hope to do. The particular problems of work and vocation for women are explored in the novel and will be discussed in the section, 'Feminism and the Novel'. In the context of a discussion of themes, it is useful to begin with the character of Ladislaw. He enters the novel as a young relative of Casaubon who has no focus or direction. He dabbles in art and journalism, flirts with the idea of taking up law, and finally becomes a politician. With his gifts of fluency, versatility and intelligence, he yet cannot identify for a long time an occupation that will give him both spiritual and practical fulfilment. The search for a vocation is reflected in Fred Vincy, who fails his exams, and waits in expectation of inheriting Featherstone's estate. When that future 'fails', he drifts through social pressure towards the clergy. Mary Garth objects to his lack of vocation first of all because he has no desire to earn a living, and later because he feels no spiritual compulsion to be a clergyman. Fred must combine the need to work with a commitment to a particular kind of work. The clergyman

Farebrother prefers his scientific hobbies to his occupation, and this is in part a warning to Fred.

Some sense of uncertainty about one's vocation seems inevitable in the contexts of social change, the gradations of social class, and the passing of time. Fred's, and Ladislaw's, search for something to do is partly a result of changing times, when the old categories of occupation and social class no longer obtain. Ladislaw is disinherited, and disinclined to take up an occupation merely for status; Fred must resist his parents' desire for him to rise socially through his education and occupation. On the other hand, Farebrother's situation represents the unavoidable effects of time on one's aspirations. To Lydgate, he says, '"I am some ten or twelve years older than you, and have come to a compromise"' (p. 202); he admits to Fred, '"I have always been too lax, and have been uneasy in consequence"' (p. 556). This combination of being in the wrong profession and resigning himself to it, is clear when, having been relieved from his financial constrictions by the gift of the Lowick living, Farebrother says to Lydgate, '"I used often to wish I had been something else than a clergyman ... but perhaps it will be better to try and make as good a clergyman out of myself as I can"' (p. 555).

Failure, or compromise, abounds in the novel. The notion of success is harder to find. Sometimes it seems that success itself is the ability to compromise, as in Farebrother's case – and in Dorothea's. It is striking that in a novel so concerned with knowledge and with the intellectual or spiritual life, the man most contented is the man who is practical, whose business has failed in the past, and who has no aspirations, either social or mental:

Caleb Garth often shook his head in meditation on the value, the indispensable might of that myriad-headed, myriad-handed labour by which the social body is fed, clothed, and housed. It had laid hold of his imagination in boyhood ... His early ambition had been to have as effective a share as possible in this sublime labour, which was peculiarly dignified by him with the name of 'business'. (p. 283)

The combination of the practical and the imaginative, as is also seen in Susan and Mary Garth, emerges as some kind of ideal success in the novel. Fred's education into Caleb's business is hard and sometimes comic, as he learns to drop his social pretensions, to write a clear hand, and to economize, but it becomes the right occupation for him, and brings him the reward, not only of fulfilment, but of a happy marriage.

David Daiches takes an extreme view of this aspect of the novel:

The Garth family are the only major characters in *Middlemarch* (apart from the ineducable Rosamond) who are not educated by experience; they do not change. This is because they are already in possession of the moral education that matters by the time the novel opens . . . the Garth family establishes the criteria to which most other actions are referred.

This view appears to be convincing in many ways. Both Dorothea and Lydgate might be described as aiming, positively, to combine practice and imagination in a Garth-like way: Dorothea wishes to act, to serve, as well as to experience spiritual goodness, and Lydgate's medical research is a combination of physical experiment and imagination. Yet they are particularly drawn to our attention because of their association with reform, change, and a questing impulse beyond present and day-to-day limitations. It is difficult to imagine the society of Middlemarch, which excludes them both, being upheld as a sensible alternative to their struggles. While both fall short and miss the settled contentment of the Garths, both are necessary to prevent a certain stagnation in the society of Middlemarch. This is an example of the way in which the novel carries a kind of 'double vision', endorsing differing, often contradictory, versions of experience.

The topic of occupation brings with it, not only the question of fulfilment and commitment, but also the pressing subject of money. Like many nineteenth-century novels, *Middlemarch* is preoccupied with money, and like many nineteenth-century novels, too, it betrays dilemmas and contradictions. At the beginning, we meet well-off characters such as Dorothea and Celia, Brooke and Sir James, who live in an aristocratic and sub-aristocratic milieu, where money is inherited, assumed and taken for granted. Brooke, the quintessential gadfly who has tried everything but stuck with nothing, has no need to earn money, being a prosperous landowner. The familiar question of responsibility is rehearsed in the contrast between Brooke's dereliction of duty as a landlord and Sir James's conscientiousness. Brooke's aimlessness is implicitly attributed to his freedom not to work, and therefore the *need* for money is proposed in a typically bourgeois manner to be focusing and benevolent. The novel does not remain for long in the Brooke/Sir James milieu, and increasingly there develops a discussion of the necessity for money. Ladislaw's indebtedness to Casaubon, which he rejects decisively, forces him to enter gainful employment; Fred's disappointment in not inheriting Featherstone's estate performs a similarly constructive function.

Middlemarch would seem, therefore, to endorse certain middle-class attitudes towards money. Certainly, as Simon Dentith detects, there is a

typical contradiction caused by a simultaneous emphasis on the importance of money, and rejection of the practical aspects of earning it.
Dentith identifies Caleb Garth's stature in the novel and his work as
instances of that contradiction:

the condition of his maintaining his dignity is that his notion of 'business'
should exclude the actual earning of money, which is a secondary and rather
sordid accident of his work. His rejection of Bulstrode's employment when he
learns the tainted source of the banker's wealth demonstrates what the separation
of 'business' from 'money' means: the cost of Caleb Garth's retaining George
Eliot's whole-hearted respect is that she should be able to distinguish the
material transformation of the world for the better which he accomplishes, from
the economic relations which in fact make such a labour possible.

According to this point of view, Caleb Garth's rejection of Bulstrode's
money is unrealistic; one cannot really ever afford such moral gestures,
least of all Garth who is running a 'business'.

Yet *Middlemarch* contains extensive debates on sums of money, both
large and small, and in the momentary glimpses of, say, the Dagleys
and the labouring people resistant to the railway, the novel does not
slide away from certain realities. Consequently, while it is difficult to
locate any single position that the author might occupy, the theme of
money, like so much else, is treated in detail.

The figures in themselves are interesting. In 1867, the official poverty
line was £60 per annum for a family.[4] Middle-class workers such as
merchants, clerks and some doctors earned between £300 and £1,000 a
year, and would keep two, three, or four servants. The upper middle-
class – businessmen, bankers and successful doctors, for example –
would earn over £1,000 a year, and would keep more than four
servants. Even allowing for a certain adjustment between 1830 and
1867, the reader is able to gauge the significance of the figures discussed
in *Middlemarch*. Fred's debt of £160 could be the full salary of a
tradesman or clerk, half the annual salary of a fairly successful middle-
class man. Farebrother struggles to support his mother, aunt and sister
in a genteel fashion on £400 a year, a salary towards the bottom of
middle-class living standards. He says that he would be glad of the £40
that taking up the post at the new infirmary would bring him. Mrs
Cadwallader is known as a thrifty person, having married beneath
her in marrying a clergyman earning only £1,000 a year: that 'only'
confirms her position among the gentry. On the other hand, Mrs
Garth has painstakingly saved £80 for her son's apprenticeship, and
Mary has heroically been able to save £24: these sums are swallowed

up in Fred's debt, even after Featherstone has given Fred a gift of £100.

Bulstrode, as banker, occupies an interesting position in the novel in this respect, particularly as he wields a supervisory power over his fellows through his ability to lend money. He translates his financial loans into spiritual bonds, lending money only to those he deems deserving, and thereafter keeping a watchful eye on their conduct. The revelation of his suppression of the existence of Sarah Dunkirk in order to keep his wife's money shows that his moral superiority is truly 'bankrupt'. Money perverts spiritual and emotional aspirations. Bulstrode becomes a focus in the text for the manipulations attendant on money. He is blackmailed by Raffles. He attempts to bribe Ladislaw, by offering him £500 a year. In this instance, the figures reveal that he is offering a reasonably comfortable way of life to Will – a significance that demonstrates his financial power, his social standing, the desperation he is experiencing, and also Will's disinterestedness.

In the network of references to money in the novel, two are particularly prominent: Dorothea's decision to marry Ladislaw, and Lydgate's debts. When Dorothea chooses to live on her £700 a year with Ladislaw, she is rejecting Casaubon's money, she is marrying a penniless man, and she will lose control of her finances in losing her status as single woman. These are all relevant matters. How are we to read her decision? In terms of the ideology of the novel, she is laudably rejecting materialism for the truth of the heart's affections, just as Ladislaw has rejected first Casaubon's, and then Bulstrode's, money, in order to retain his independence, and in order not to be indebted to men whom he cannot respect; it is in the context of these decisions that Lydgate's acceptance of Bulstrode's money becomes culpably irresponsible. In fact, rejection of financial ties may be read as an index of independence from the Middlemarch ethos. Arnold Kettle comments that 'It is Dorothea alone who, with Ladislaw, successfully rebels against the Middlemarch values', and these two characters are notable for their habits of refusing or giving away money. At the beginning of the novel we have been told that Dorothea

was regarded as an heiress, for not only had the sisters seven hundred a-year each from their parents, but if Dorothea married and had a son, that son would inherit Mr Brooke's estate, presumably worth about three thousand a-year – a rental which seemed wealth to provincial families, still discussing Mr Peel's late conduct on the Catholic Question, innocent of future gold-fields, and of that gorgeous plutocracy which has so nobly exalted the necessities of genteel life. (p. 31)

Dorothea's decision is controversial not because of the possibility that Will is a fortune-hunter – Casaubon's precautions are ridiculed in the text, and Will's disinterestedness has been proved – but because £700 is on the cusp between middle-class and upper middle-class existence. And here the full complexity of the situation becomes evident. The first page of the novel contains the information that 'the Brooke connections, though not exactly aristocratic, were unquestionably "good"' (p. 29). Dorothea is choosing to live on an annual sum of money that designates middle-class existence. At the end of the novel, Brooke reports that he has said to her, '"you don't know what it is to live on seven hundred a-year, and have no carriage, and that kind of thing, and go amongst people who don't know who you are"' (pp. 874–5), and Celia, who has married into the aristocracy, says to her, '"How can you always live in a street? And you will be so poor"' (p. 879). These comments seem to convey two things: the genuine change and loss of comfort that Dorothea is embracing, which call forth our sympathy, and an ironic perception of the limited horizons that can regard such living conditions as horrific.

The swoops of Lydgate's fortunes are even more tellingly detailed, and are bound up with issues of social class, material success, and spiritual failure. Lydgate's practice is notionally worth £800, but he has soon accumulated debts to the amount of £1,000, caused by the unthinking establishment of his married home. He finds himself telling Rosamond that they must try to live within £400 a year, dismiss two of their three servants and keep only one horse. Lydgate has disregarded the apparent trivia of the cost of things in a lordly manner. Meanwhile, Rosamond wishes to be seen to be living in comparative style. With a limited income, their combined attitudes hasten financial disaster. The careful analysis of Lydgate's financial problems directs attention to the carelessness of those who do not think about money: in this respect, the commentary is radical in its criticism of the moneyed. However, the main insight afforded by Lydgate's difficulties is that the need for money often determines actions and possibilities:

Lydgate was aware that his concessions to Rosamond were often little more than the lapse of slackening resolution, the creeping paralysis apt to seize an enthusiasm which is out of adjustment to a constant portion of our lives. And on Lydgate's enthusiasm there was constantly pressing not a simple weight of sorrow, but the biting presence of a petty degrading care, such as casts the blight of irony over all higher effort.
. . . Lydgate was in debt; and he could not succeed in keeping out of his mind for long together that he was every day getting deeper into that swamp . . . (pp. 632–3).

Money-cares – debt, bankruptcy, bribery, blackmail, gambling and saving – are middle-class preoccupations in *Middlemarch*. Within the fine mesh of social gradations and in the thwarting of vocation, those money-cares are shown to be frighteningly powerful, affecting individuals in every area of their lives, from the people they mix with to their innermost feelings and thoughts. Dorothea's journey towards altruism is implicitly a luxury that she can afford, but the pressures of class and money are by no means ignored in the novel. Indeed, Dorothea herself recognizes her leisure and consciously chooses a life of less material well-being: "'I will learn what everything costs'" (p. 870). Yet even here, there is possibly an authorial irony in Dorothea's *need* to learn, while at the same time, her willingness to learn the metaphoric cost of her decision is applauded.

3. Characters and Characterization

The protean relation of the narrator to her characters is one of the crucial points about characterization in *Middlemarch*. It would be difficult to discuss characters in isolation, as if they were independent of an authorial perspective. Simon Dentith notes that 'Many passages of the novel are marked by a complex irony which often works against the characters but which can modulate into agreement or solidarity.' Derek Oldfield has commented, 'George Eliot makes her point by zig-zagging. We oscillate between an emotional identification with a character and an obliquely judicious response to their situation.'[5] This critical agreement about the shifts between irony and sympathy, however, becomes an equally frequent critical dissent in discussions of Dorothea and Ladislaw, as we shall see.

An example of the way in which characters sporadically enjoy the sympathy of their creator, and then just as swiftly become targets of ironic commentary, may be seen in the use of the adjective 'poor' by the narrator. Hand in hand with the narrator's relation to her characters goes her relationship with her readers, who are drawn into a responsive and collusive point of view. When Lydgate is described at the end of Chapter 70 as 'Poor Lydgate! the "if Rosamond will not mind", which had fallen from him involuntarily as part of his thought, was a significant mark of the yoke he bore' (p. 768), both narrator and reader understand the sympathy that is due to him, for both have followed him through a succession of frustrations and disappointments. When Dorothea is called 'Poor Dorothea' after Casaubon has rejected her well-meaning suggestion that some financial restitution is due to Ladislaw (p. 410), there is similar agreement between narrator and reader that she deserves compassion at this point. Yet sometimes the same adjective implies a greater distance between narrator and character. For instance, at the onset of Fred's illness,

Mr Wrench did not neglect sending the usual white parcels, which this time had black and drastic contents. Their effect was not alleviating to poor Fred, who, however, unwilling as he said to believe that he was 'in for an illness', rose at his usual hour the next morning and went downstairs meaning to breakfast, but succeeded in nothing but in sitting and shivering by the fire. (p. 292)

While there is some sympathy here for a young man who is feeling unwell, there is also some humour at the notion that Wrench's 'drastic' physic does nothing to 'alleviate' Fred. Such relatively gentle irony becomes more problematic in the case of Mrs Bulstrode when she is faced with the realization of her husband's disgrace. Mrs Plymdale feels a somewhat uncharacteristic sympathy for her friend:

The sharp little woman's conscience was somewhat troubled in the adjustment of these opposing 'bests' and of her griefs and satisfactions under late events, which were likely to humble those who needed humbling, but also to fall heavily on her old friend whose faults she would have preferred seeing on a background of prosperity. (p. 802)

This friendly concern is followed by an authorial perspective: 'Poor Mrs Bulstrode, meanwhile, had been no further shaken by the oncoming tread of calamity than in the busier stirring of that secret uneasiness which had always been present in her since the last visit of Raffles to The Shrubs.' Mrs Bulstrode is in ignorance of what everyone else in Middlemarch is talking about, and the state of her ignorance foreshadows a gathering grief for her. The dramatic irony wavers between compassion and a tendency to smile at the composure of an as yet unknowing victim.

The narrator's superior knowledge is imparted to the reader at the expense of characters even more noticeably when she says, 'Poor Lydgate! or shall I say, Poor Rosamond! Each lived in a world of which the other knew nothing' (p. 195). In the case of Rosamond this can, and often does, modulate into a laugh at the character's predicament: for example, when Mrs Bulstrode asks Rosamond if she is actually engaged to Lydgate, 'Poor Rosamond's feelings were very unpleasant' (p. 331), for of course she cannot truthfully reply that she is. However, perhaps towards the end, when Rosamond imagines that with Bulstrode's money there can be a new beginning after so many tribulations, only to discover the extent of Lydgate's associated disgrace, sympathy prevails over irony in the narrator's tone: 'soon the sky became black over poor Rosamond' (p. 811).

Such nuances of tone are most difficult to gauge in the presentation of Casaubon and Dorothea. There is straightforward humour (but perhaps a hint of compassion) in: 'Poor Mr Casaubon had imagined that his long studious bachelorhood had stored up for him a compound interest of enjoyment, and that large drafts on his affections would not fail to be honoured' (p. 111); the metaphor of saving here confirms the folly of his imagination. But he is accorded a kinder understanding when the degree of his lonely doubt is made clear:

> Poor Mr Casaubon was distrustful of everybody's feeling towards him, especially as a husband. To let any one suppose that he was jealous would be to admit their (suspected) view of his disadvantages: to let them know that he did not find marriage particularly blissful would imply his conversion to their (probably) earlier disapproval ... All through his life Mr Casaubon had been trying not to admit even to himself the inward sores of self-doubt and jealousy. (p. 412)

Dorothea is often described as 'poor', yet it remains unclear quite how we are to read such epithets. Are they the narrator's assessment, for example, or Dorothea's own self-pity or self-dramatization? The comment in Chapter 20, 'Poor Dorothea! she was certainly troublesome – to herself chiefly; but this morning for the first time she had been troublesome to Mr Casaubon' (p. 230), simultaneously laughs at Dorothea's personal anxiety and points to Casaubon's unreasonable inflexibility towards her. When Brooke says to her, in trying to persuade her to think more carefully about agreeing to marry Casaubon, '"It *is* a noose, you know. Temper, now. There is temper. And a husband likes to be master"' (p. 64), Dorothea's response is: '"I know that I must expect trials, uncle. Marriage is a state of higher duties. I never thought of it as mere personal ease," said poor Dorothea.' If we feel unalloyed sympathy with her at this point, we recognize the incomprehension that she suffers from others as she attempts to make her life a noble one. But if we concur with some of the views of Dorothea expressed by other characters – that, for instance, she is misled – then there is irony in her ignorance of the realities of marriage, irony in her youthful eagerness for 'trials', and a poverty in her mental landscape. 'Poor Dorothea' here can suggest both compassion *and* irony.

One way of explaining the elusive tone of the narrator towards her characters is to look briefly at the early essay, 'The Natural History of German Life' (1856). In this, George Eliot praises the German writer Riehl, for depicting peasant life in Germany in a realistic manner, and for providing a 'natural history' of the peasantry. George Eliot's approbation of objective observation is clarified when she says:

> The greatest benefit we owe to the artist, whether painter, poet, or novelist, is the extension of our sympathies. Appeals founded on generalizations and statistics require a sympathy ready-made, a moral sentiment already in activity; but a picture of human life such as a great artist can give, surprises even the trivial and the selfish into that attention to what is apart from themselves, which may be called the raw material of moral sentiment.

The 'extension of our sympathies' is wrought by such realism. A

115

'natural history' of 'what is apart from' the reader, implies a considerable distance between the author and reader, and the subjects or characters under examination. This is particularly the case in earlier novels such as *Adam Bede* (commonly thought to owe its portrayal of farming people to the ideas in 'The Natural History of German Life') and *The Mill on the Floss*. In *Middlemarch*, we may be struck by the comparison between Mrs Cadwallader and a creature in a water-drop under the microscope, or by the linking of the mourners at Featherstone's funeral with animals going into the Ark; groups of people are occasionally placed as zoological specimens. But more importantly, the function of 'natural history' in *Middlemarch* consists in moral understanding. This paradox, between objectivity and identification, is confirmed in the words of the critic, U. C. Knoepflmacher, who says that the novel 'contains a scrupulous "scientific" dissection of character by a writer hostile to the aims of science', but also observes that 'It is noteworthy that George Eliot inverts the order in *Middlemarch* by giving supremacy to the non-scientific, but imaginative, Dorothea.'[6]

The word 'character' can mean, among several things, both those qualities that go to make up an individual's personality, and an individual's personality considered especially in relation to honesty, reliability and goodness. 'Character' therefore semantically shifts from being description to being moral assessment. It could be argued that George Eliot, unlike some other nineteenth-century writers, refuses to make her characters wholly good or wholly bad. It is equally accurate to say that to her, character is morally significant. She is ironic in describing Bulstrode's characteristic way of dealing with people:

Mr Bulstrode had ... a deferential bending attitude in listening, and an apparently fixed attentiveness in his eyes which made those persons who thought themselves worth hearing infer that he was seeking the utmost improvement from their discourse. Others, who expected to make no great figure, disliked this kind of moral lantern turned on them. If you are not proud of your cellar, there is no thrill of satisfaction in seeing your guest hold up his wine-glass to the light and look judicial. Such joys are reserved for conscious merit. (p. 151)

However, George Eliot certainly turns a 'moral lantern' on her characters, although her moral judgements are always cast in the context of compassion as well as objective inquiry. Moral generosity also derives from her equally scientific conviction, relying on evolutionary theory, that 'character . . . is a process and an unfolding' (p. 178). This comment occurs in a discussion of Lydgate, where the development of the individual through time, and the mixed lights of the individual, are both stressed.

The man was still in the making, as much as the Middlemarch doctor and immortal discoverer, and there were both virtues and faults capable of shrinking or expanding. The faults will not, I hope, be a reason for the withdrawal of your interest in him. Among our valued friends is there not some one or other who is a little too self-confident and disdainful; whose distinguished mind is a little spotted with commonness; who is a little pinched here and protuberant there with native prejudices; or whose better energies are liable to lapse down the wrong channel under the influence of transient solicitations? (pp. 178–9)

An appeal here to the reader's experience of human nature works to broaden response and interest, yet the language also remains unremittingly moral: 'virtues', 'faults', 'better energies', 'lapse'.

Characters in *Middlemarch*, then, are placed and read by the narrator constantly: often in a comprehending way, and sometimes remorselessly. Within this dominating authorial voice, how are they portrayed? *Middlemarch* is posited on a world of interaction and interdependence. There is a tension between individuality and community, and an equal tension in authorial focus between personality and human nature. Walter Pater, writing at the same time as George Eliot was composing *Middlemarch*, and subject to many of the same currents of thought, mourned the loss of former certitudes in his 'Conclusion' to *The Renaissance*:

birth and gesture and death and the springing of violets from the grave are but a few out of ten thousand resultant combinations. That clear, perpetual outline of face and limb is but an image of ours, under which we group them – a design in a web, the actual threads of which pass out beyond it. This at least of flame-like our life has, that it is but the concurrence, renewed from moment to moment, of forces parting sooner or later on their ways.

While Pater and Eliot share a sense of change, Pater emphasizes transience, and Eliot continues to affirm meaningfulness. However, the mere 'image' of individuality, caught in a larger web and constantly losing identity by being implicated in the web, which Pater describes – 'a design in a web, the actual threads of which pass out beyond it' – is a formulation that is helpful when discussing character in *Middlemarch*. Individuals are caught up in a social medium that threatens the ego and that also demolishes the significance of singular character.

This is the case, too, in characterization as 'image'. It is a common technique of characterization to describe the physical appearance and demeanour of an individual. In fact, it has even been suggested that the emphasis on appearance in nineteenth-century fiction is more significant than the twentieth-century reader might suppose: 'few people nowadays would argue that the face is a particularly useful indicator of character, whereas many writers of the last century had at least a residual belief in physiognomy or phrenology'.[7] In the light of this comment, George Eliot's treatment of appearance and physique may well be more significant than we are inclined to realize. She positively pleads for Casaubon against his unprepossessing looks:

I protest against all our interest, all our effort at understanding being given to the young skins that look blooming in spite of trouble; for these too will get faded, and will know the older and more eating griefs which we are helping to neglect. In spite of the blinking eyes and white moles objectionable to Celia, and the want of muscular curve which was morally painful to Sir James, Mr Casaubon had an intense consciousness within him, and was spiritually a-hungered like the rest of us. (p. 312)

The disjunction between outward appearance and inner reality is made more piercing in a context of 'residual belief in physiognomy or phrenology'. This is underlined in the case of Rosamond. She is so pretty that Lydgate allows himself to believe in her goodness:

She blushed and looked at him as the garden flowers look at us when we walk forth happily among them in the transcendent evening light: is there not a soul beyond utterance, half-nymph, half-child, in those delicate petals which glow and breathe about the centres of deep colour? (p. 386)

This passage shows Lydgate's sentimental and conventional attitudes towards women. It also works to remind us that there is definitely not 'a soul beyond utterance' within Rosamond. What she looks like is in direct contradiction to the monstrous egoism that is lurking within. Her prettiness is thematically significant, too, in that it becomes her artillery of disdain when arguing with Lydgate later.

Pater's 'clear, perpetual outline of face and limb' may exist in the text of *Middlemarch*, but the relevance of physical details to the shifting subjectivity within is scrutinized sternly. Similarly, the attributes of 'voice' are treated in a complex manner in the novel. On the whole, characters do have tones and timbres in their voices that seem to signify character. Yet this is contradicted when the narrator discusses Bulstrode:

Do not imagine his sickly aspect to have been of the yellow, black-haired sort: he had a pale blond skin, thin grey-besprinkled brown hair, light-grey eyes, and a large forehead. Loud men called his subdued tone an undertone, and sometimes implied that it was inconsistent with openness; though there seems to be no reason why a loud man should not be given to concealment of anything except his own voice, unless it can be shown that Holy Writ has placed the seat of candour in the lungs. (p. 151)

The relativity of judgement available here pulls away from any certainty of interpretation.

A moral hierarchy is implicit in George Eliot's project, yet the characters have both virtues and faults. Two minor characters in particular are used to contradict any facile moral assessment: Mr Brooke and Farebrother. Brooke, it may be observed from a close reading, is unfocused, superficial and uncommitted, in ways that are condemned in parallel characters such as Fred Vincy, Ladislaw and even Lydgate at times; he is at fault in standing as a candidate for Reform yet being a negligent landlord. In his meandering contributions to conversation he is often portrayed comically. However, his apparently harmless and unconsidered remarks often prove to be accurate, and part of his role is to be unwittingly perspicacious. To Mrs Cadwallader, he says, '"there is no part of the county where opinion is narrower than it is here"' (p. 78); to Casaubon, '"you must teach my niece to take things more quietly, eh, Dorothea?"' (p. 90), and at the end of the novel:

'Well, you know, Chettam,' said Mr Brooke, good-humouredly, nursing his leg, 'I can't turn my back on Dorothea. I must be a father to her up to a certain point. I said, "My dear, I won't refuse to give you away." I had spoken strongly before. But I can cut off the entail, you know. It will cost money and be troublesome; but I can do it, you know.'

Mr Brooke nodded at Sir James, and felt that he was both showing his own force of resolution and propitiating what was just in the Baronet's vexation. He had hit on a more ingenious mode of parrying than he was aware of. He had touched a motive of which Sir James was ashamed. (p. 876)

Farebrother, too, often reflects that aspect of the novel that examines the concept of vocation. A clergyman who prefers his scientific pursuits, and is in the wrong career, perhaps, he is also fond of the gambling table, which links him to those characters who lack control, like Fred, or who value money above honour, like Bulstrode. Yet he becomes a noble figure of compromise, combining his scientific classification and his clerical duties, delivering honest sermons, looking after his mother, aunt and sister, while foregoing the possibility of pressing his suit with Mary Garth. His advice, to both Lydgate and Fred, may be born of failure, but it is directed fruitfully and selflessly.

The way that the characters in *Middlemarch* only exist within their author's controlling moral framework, however shifting that framework may be, becomes a critical problem with the characters of Dorothea and Ladislaw. Both appear to have eluded the author's scrupulous irony, and to be presented, technically and thematically, with surprising idealism. Dorothea's ardour and selflessness, Ladislaw's youth and promise, are not questioned to the same extent as are the hopes, aspirations, and inner ruminations of other characters. Nor are they fully realized in presentation: the narrator frequently resorts to describing them as 'child-like', as if to convey in a sentimental manner some quality of innocence. Many critics have registered a discomfort about these characters and their characterization in these terms. Henry James argued that

The figure of Will Ladislaw is a beautiful attempt, with many finely completed points; but on the whole it seems to us a failure. It is the only eminent failure in the book, and its defects are therefore the more striking . . . The author, who is evidently very fond of him, has found for him here and there some charming and eloquent touches; but in spite of these he remains vague and impalpable to the end. He is, we may say, the one figure which a masculine intellect of the same power as George Eliot's would not have conceived with the same complacency; he is, in short, roughly speaking, a woman's man.

The author's partiality for Ladislaw and the unfocused characterization have been cited as flaws ever since. Throughout the first half of the novel, he has to function as the beckoning alternative to Casaubon for Dorothea, and, as will be discussed in the section on 'Imagery', this function is often structured in semi-allegorical ways.

Reactions to Dorothea are more numerous and more varied. F. R. Leavis, in *The Great Tradition*, provided readers with the most extreme and least tolerant view:

Dorothea . . . is a product of George Eliot's own 'soul-hunger' – another daydream ideal self. This persistence, in the midst of so much that is so other, of an unreduced enclave of the old immaturity is disconcerting in the extreme. We have an alternation between the poised impersonal insight of a finely tempered wisdom and something like the emotional confusions and self-importances of adolescence.

Leavis bases his strictures on an absence of irony in George Eliot's attitude towards Dorothea, but he also discounts Dorothea's idealism as George Eliot's 'emotional confusions and self-importances of adolescence'. Any discussion of Dorothea depends greatly on the reader's response to irony, and on how far that reader discerns irony in the portrayal. Laurence Lerner has argued that a response to Dorothea relies equally on how much the reader values such spiritual ambition: it is, he claims, held up in the text as something to be admired. Therefore, while Dorothea may be comically mistaken at the beginning (and here close reading locates nuances of sympathy and irony), her struggles against an uncomprehending social circle invite sadness rather than scorn from the reader.[8] This interpretation rests on an analysis of the portrayal of Dorothea as potentially ironic, but also ambiguous, revealing the nobility of her enterprise as well as the comic mismatch of desire to circumstance.

On the other hand, the 'problem' of Dorothea has been resolved by other critics in quite different ways. David Daiches prefers a version of *Middlemarch* which emphasizes its ironic tone. He points to Dorothea's enthusiasms at the beginning and goes so far as to suggest that we are intended to see Dorothea's ardour as sublimated sexuality – a sublimation of which she is unaware, while the reader perceives it. This produces a high degree of dramatic irony in the presentation of Dorothea in the early chapters. Consequently, Daiches reaches the position of arguing that Mary Garth, with her qualities of common sense, plainness, integrity and self-discipline, 'is closest to the moral centre of the novel and closest to the author herself'. Like Leavis, Daiches shows a fondness for inserting his own version of George Eliot into the text itself, and he transforms *Middlemarch* into a novel that extols the virtues of the Garths at the expense of spiritual or visionary dimensions to life. A different point of view is expressed by Arnold Kettle, who says that the incursion of the spiritual into the novel, which on the whole is committed to the ordinary and the prosaic, is problematic:

Dorothea represents that element in human experience for which in the determinist universe of mechanistic materialism there is no place – the need of man to change the world that he inherits. Dorothea is the force that she is in the novel precisely because she encompasses this vital motive-force in human life; and she fails ultimately to convince us because in George Eliot's conscious philosophy she has no place.

This is persuasive, but short of cynicism, the reader must respond to what is evidently intended as a central experience of the novel: the presence of far-seeing, progressive individuals caught in a provincial society in 1830. Lydgate, Dorothea and Ladislaw all eventually leave Middlemarch for London, and carry the novel into the future.

4. Imagery

The linguistic texture of *Middlemarch* is permeated with a developed series of images. Some of these images – most notably of water and light – are traditional, wide-ranging and common in Western culture, drawing on associations such as fertility, growth, baptism and enlightenment. In their careful and extended use here, they press into service the breadth of scientific, literary and historical allusions also characteristic of the novel.

Imagery is one of the dominant modes of the authorial voice. Using highly metaphorical language, the narrator familiarizes, generalizes and makes concrete the individual action. J. Hillis Miller suggests that *Middlemarch* shows a 'recognition of the irreducibly figurative or metaphorical nature of all language', and that this becomes a theme in the novel: 'Seeing is always interpretation, that is, what is seen is always taken as a sign standing for something else, as an emblem, a hieroglyph, a parable.'[9] Certainly, the textuality of the novel and its high quotient of imagery both lead to observations on the relativity of knowledge. In addition, imagery helps to link the thematic parallels between the separate strands, or stories, of *Middlemarch*. The narrative is preoccupied, as Gillian Beer says in *Darwin's Plots*, with relations, variations, and, we might add, substitutions.

A critical discussion of imagery, by laying bare a skeleton of linguistic texture, often risks reducing the subliminal to the programmatic. It is important to recognize that the imagery in *Middlemarch*, while consistent, is not often insistent. It is so embedded in the commentary, dialogue, action, and psychological and moral complexity that our reading experience is not just alert to the imagery alone.

An obvious starting point is with Miss *Brooke*, whose name has an association with water. It is an association that is present throughout the novel, from the cygnet among ducks which 'never finds the living stream in fellowship with its own oary-footed kind' in the Prelude (p. 26) to the personality that 'spent itself in channels which had no great name on the earth' of the Finale (p. 896). Water brings fertility, energy and refreshment, and is often the metaphoric medium in which characters would ideally move and have their being. For example, Mrs Cadwallader is described by means of an analogy with a creature in water:

Even with a microscope directed on a water-drop we find ourselves making interpretations which turn out to be rather coarse; for whereas under a weak lens you may seem to see a creature exhibiting an active voracity into which other smaller creatures actively play as if they were so many animated tax-pennies, a stronger lens reveals to you certain tiniest hairlets which make vortices for these victims while the ˹wallower waits passively at his receipt of custom. In this way, metaphorically speaking, a strong lens applied to Mrs Cadwallader's matchmaking will show a play of minute causes ... (p. 83)

Here, metaphor slides from a water-drop to 'tax-pennies' momentarily; scientific and evolutionary aspects dominate the water imagery, and the narrator's role as investigative scientist is touched upon. Sally Shuttleworth draws attention to the way that metaphor can coexist with current language of the late 1860s when she says, 'The recurrent imagery of flowing water and streams ... is not simply metaphoric in origin but is grounded in contemporary social and psychological theories of energy flow.' Metaphor allows complex fields of semantic association to develop, and this works noticeably in *Middlemarch*. Lydgate, for example, in a crucial passage about his potential future at the time when he arrives in Middlemarch, is described as a swimmer:

He was at a starting-point which makes many a man's career a fine subject for betting, if there were any gentlemen given to that amusement who could appreciate the complicated probabilities of an arduous purpose, with all the possible thwartings and furtherings of circumstance, all the niceties of inward balance, by which a man swims and makes his point or else is carried headlong. (p. 178)

Is he going to swim or be 'carried headlong'? After his first social visit to Vincy's, he returns home and reads until very late, as yet unseduced by Rosamond's charms except in a superficial way:

As he threw down his book, stretched his legs towards the embers in the grate, and clasped his hands at the back of his head, in that agreeable after-glow of excitement when thought lapses from examination of a specific object into a suffusive sense of its connections with all the rest of our existence – seems, as it were, to throw itself on its back after vigorous swimming and float with the repose of unexhausted strength – Lydgate felt a triumphant delight in his studies ... (p. 194)

However, much later the image of swimming is picked up and given a different twist. His circumstances are described as being 'as noxious to him as an inlet of mud to a creature that has been used to breathe and bathe and dart after its illuminated prey in the clearest of waters' (p. 631). Lydgate is now a 'creature' in an evolutionary scenario, finding himself in an inappropriate environment and locked into struggle (sounded in 'prey'). He can no longer swim with ease or enjoyment. Turning to Rosamond, her 'moment of naturalness' which precipitates their engagement is when 'she felt that her tears had risen, and it was no use to try to do anything else than let them stay like water on a blue flower or let them fall over her cheeks, even as they would' (p. 335). The image of Rosamond as a 'torpedo', already discussed, links evolutionary struggle in the marriage with the pervasive water imagery, too, and throws into question the concept of human 'nature' in the novel.

It is in Dorothea's story that water imagery plays its most important part. She has a great need to 'pour forth her girlish and womanly feeling' (p. 230); she cries frequently at the beginning of the novel: through excess of emotion, through frustration that she is expected to marry Sir James, through disappointment at the reality of Casaubon's personality in Rome. But like water, that can be formless and overwhelming, her emotions, enthusiasm and sensitivity need to be directed and channelled. There is a telling exchange in Chapter 7:

'When we were coming home from Lausanne my uncle took us to hear the great organ at Freiburg, and it made me sob.'
'That kind of thing is not healthy, my dear,' said Mr Brooke. (p. 90)

Mr Brooke is also appositely named, for his energies meander and dissipate themselves through lack of direction. Yet he provides the voice of reason here, warning Dorothea of too indulgent a response. Faced with the bewildering lack of response in Casaubon, her 'ideas and resolves seemed like melting ice floating and lost in the warm flood of which they had been but another form' (p. 230), and she is in danger of 'drowning' in self-pity alone in the Roman apartment. But this significant chapter ends with another watery image:

in Dorothea's mind there was a current into which all thought and feeling were apt sooner or later to flow – the reaching forward of the whole consciousness towards the fullest truth, the least partial good. There was clearly something better than anger and despondency. (p. 235)

The 'current' here, which flows with energy and direction, is later taken up as an image of electricity, as will be seen.

The mismatch between Dorothea and Casaubon is conveyed adroitly and even comically by the authorial comment that Casaubon

determined to abandon himself to the stream of feeling, and perhaps was surprised to find what an exceedingly shallow rill it was. As in droughty regions baptism by immersion could only be performed symbolically, so Mr Casaubon found that sprinkling was the utmost approach to a plunge which his stream would afford him. (p. 87)

Casaubon is here linked to rituals of baptism, appropriate to his researches into mythology and primitive societies. But he himself remains dried up and shrivelled within his egoism, '"no better than a mummy"' (p. 81) in the words of Sir James. In Rome, Dorothea's realization of Casaubon's limitations is compared with the discovery that 'the sea is not within sight – that, in fact, you are exploring an enclosed basin' (p. 228), and images of stagnant water, swamps and marshes surround this character in the text. There is another ironic counterpoint in Casaubon's desiccated discussion of 'the Philistine god Dagon and other fish-deities' (p. 228). His responses 'had long shrunk to a sort of dried preparation, a lifeless embalmment of knowledge' (p. 229).

While Dorothea is associated with water, Casaubon is frequently described in terms of another set of imagery, first introduced ironically at Dorothea's expense:

He was all she had at first imagined him to be: almost everything he had said seemed like a specimen from a mine, or the inscription on the door of a museum which might open on the treasures of past ages . . . (p. 55)

Her veneration of age and authority contains within it the premonition of Casaubon's sterility and associations with enclosed spaces, empty rooms and the underworld. In another episode that shows Dorothea's naïvety, 'Mr Casaubon apparently did not care about building cottages, and diverted the talk to the extremely narrow accommodation which was to be had in the dwellings of the ancient Egyptians' (p. 56), thereby demonstrating to the reader, if not to Dorothea at this point, the narrowness of his own horizons. Images of constriction and stoniness accumulate, as when 'she drove with Mr Casaubon to the Vatican, walked with him through the stony avenue of inscriptions, and . . . parted with him at the entrance to the Library' (p. 234), the library becoming implicated here in an associative web with monuments, tablets and gravestones.

The 'extremely narrow accommodation' of the ancient Egyptians shifts to encompass images such as the labyrinth of the Minotaur, another mythological reference point, and one which reflects the dimness of Casaubon's mental processes:

Poor Mr Casaubon himself was lost among small closets and winding stairs, and in an agitated dimness about the Cabeiri, or in an exposure of other mythologists' ill-considered parallels, easily lost sight of any purpose which had prompted him to these labours. With his taper stuck before him he forgot the absence of windows, and in bitter manuscript remarks on other men's notions about the solar deities, he had become indifferent to the sunlight. (p. 229–30)

It is useful to pause at this passage, for it is remarkably rich in metaphors that recur in other areas of the novel, thus linking Casaubon into the greater texture of *Middlemarch*. The 'small closets and winding stairs' remind the reader of labyrinths and prisons, and Casaubon's use of a taper conveys his pathetic lack of enlightenment or insight into his subject. The 'absence of windows' touches on a contrast throughout the novel between individuals regarding mirrors and looking out of windows at other people, while the reference to solar deities and sunlight demonstrates Casaubon's inability to relate his reading to experience, and introduces an idea of a sun-god, which Ladislaw is to represent to the entrapped Dorothea. As Casaubon 'easily lost sight of any purpose', the reader might recall the later portrayal of 'purpose' in Rosamond and Dorothea. This accumulation of fields of metaphoric reference works intricately throughout the novel.

When Dorothea returns to Lowick as the new Mrs Casaubon, she brings 'an incongruous renewal of life and glow' to the old-fashioned boudoir which is to become a prison of solitude and aimlessness (p. 306). Even the view from the window is at this point a 'still, white enclosure which made her visible world' (p. 307). Images of constriction, coldness and darkness multiply in the text: 'The duties of her married life, contemplated as so great beforehand, seemed to be shrinking with the furniture and the white vapour-walled landscape' (p. 307), and:

Her blooming full-pulsed youth stood there in a moral imprisonment which made itself one with the chill, colourless, narrowed landscape, with the shrunken furniture, the never-read books, and the ghostly stag in a pale fantastic world that seemed to be vanishing from the daylight.

In the first minutes when Dorothea looked out she felt nothing but the dreary oppression ... All existence seemed to beat with a lower pulse than her own, and her religious faith was a solitary cry, the struggle out of a nightmare in which every object was withering and shrinking away from her. Each remembered thing in the room was disenchanted, was deadened as an unlit transparency ... (pp. 307–8)

Dorothea here is very like the captured Persephone, forced to spend a certain number of months with Hades in the underworld, her absence from life blighting the world with winter.

Two things happen to Dorothea: she increasingly looks out of her window at the world, and gradually comes into sympathetic communion with a wider world, and she meets Ladislaw, who brings light and warmth to the doors of her prison, rather like Orpheus who attempted to rescue Eurydice from the underworld. Ladislaw is associated with youth, movement and the sun, as well as being inclined to be musical (Orpheus being the god of music, Apollo the god of the sun):

Will Ladislaw's smile was delightful, unless you were angry with him beforehand: it was a gush of inward light illuminating the transparent skin as well as the eyes, and playing about every curve and line as if some Ariel were touching them with a new charm, and banishing for ever the traces of moodiness. (pp. 237–8)

Later, when Ladislaw goes to Lowick church in the hope of meeting Dorothea, his walk through the countryside raises many associations with spring, warmth, and music:

Will went along with a small book under his arm and a hand in each 'de-pocket, never reading, but chanting a little, as he made scenes of what would happen in church and coming out. He was experimenting in tunes to suit some words of his own, sometimes trying a ready-made melody, sometimes improvising . . .

Sometimes, when he took off his hat, shaking his head backward, and showing his delicate throat as he sang, he looked like an incarnation of the spring whose spirit filled the air – a bright creature, abundant in uncertain promises. (p. 512)

At this point, Ladislaw is less a realistic character in a novel, than a necessary mythological figure in the triad of Casaubon/Hades, Dorothea/Persephone/Eurydice, and Ladislaw/Orpheus/Apollo. The passage is only just redeemed from sentimentality by the ironic comment that the promises with which he is abundant are 'uncertain', reminding the reader of Ladislaw's lack of vocation and direction.

It is apposite to observe here that not only does the narrator use highly metaphoric language, but the characters also tend, according to their dispositions, to cast their perceptions in similes and images. And that tendency to draw analogies is subject to considerable irony, for it often shows egoism at work. Ladislaw sees the relationship between Casaubon and Dorothea in only slightly heightened versions of the mythological allusions already discussed:

'You talk as if you had never known any youth. It is monstrous – as if you had had a vision of Hades in your childhood, like the boy in the legend. You have been brought up in some of those horrible notions that choose the sweetest women to devour – like Minotaurs. And now you will go and be shut up in that stone prison at Lowick: you will be buried alive. It makes me savage to think of

it! I would rather never have seen you than think of you with such a prospect.'
(p. 253)

Ladislaw is passionate and given to hyperbole. He casts himself as a
heroic saviour by implication, and the text finally confirms that role.
There is, therefore, an underlying commentary that all experience is
inevitably subjective, and there is a sliding between ironic portrayal and
idealistic statement, as occurs to a lesser extent with Dorothea. Bulstrode and Rosamond are to refer their experience to the same metaphoric model, with even greater ironic results.

Water, prison, window and light imagery combine in a final, highly
charged, and highly idealized episode in the novel: the occasion when
Dorothea and Ladislaw eventually reach an understanding. It could, in
fact, be argued that when the text moves away from realism towards
imagery to such an extent, it loses its immediacy and becomes far more
dependent on the reader's automatic response to conventional images.
This would also help to explain the 'problem' about the characterization
of Dorothea and Ladislaw, already discussed in the section on 'Characters and Characterization'. When Ladislaw comes to Dorothea in the
library in Chapter 83, the interview commences with Dorothea standing
in the centre of the room. After some awkwardness, she moves towards
the window, commenting on the imminent storm:

They stood silent, not looking at each other, but looking at the evergreens which
were being tossed, and were showing the pale underside of their leaves against
the blackening sky. Will never enjoyed the prospect of a storm so much: it
delivered him from the necessity of going away. Leaves and little branches were
hurled about, and the thunder was getting nearer. The light was more and more
sombre, but there came a flash of lightning which made them start and look at
each other, and then smile. (pp. 867–8)

The 'blackening sky', the 'evergreens' and the paleness of the leaves are
all reminders of the presence of Casaubon, which is about to be swept
away by youth, light and warmth. Light and energy come with the
electricity of lightning (converting those 'currents' of water into channels
of force), and eventually 'the rain began to pour down' (p. 868),
releasing the emotion that has been pent up between them. Most of the
conversation takes place as Dorothea and Ladislaw gaze out at the
weather and the world hand in hand, rather than looking at each other.
And Dorothea finally speaks with 'the flood of her young passion
bearing down all the obstructions which had kept her silent' (p. 870).

The changing relationships of Casaubon, Dorothea and Ladislaw
rest on a series of metaphoric contrasts: coldness and warmth, sterility

and life, death and youth, imprisonment and liberty – but most centrally, darkness and light. The idea of Ladislaw bringing light to the darkness which Dorothea experiences with Casaubon is ironically foreshadowed in her naïve prediction about Casaubon:

since the time was gone by for guiding visions and spiritual directors, since prayer heightened yearning but not instruction, what lamp was there but knowledge? Surely learned men kept the only oil; and who more learned than Mr Casaubon? (pp. 112–13)

This should be read alongside Celia's small-minded but penetrating observation that she 'had become less afraid of "saying things" to Dorothea since this engagement; cleverness seemed to her more pitiable than ever' (p. 108). And while Dorothea yearns for enlightenment, the imagery shows at this point of the novel that she is truly benighted and blinded by her egoism, naïvety and ardour. Short-sighted, she is 'blind' to nearby minutiae of reality, but aims to be visionary. Celia tells her, '" you went on as you always do, never looking just where you are, and treading in the wrong place"' (p. 59). Yet Dorothea's ability to imagine and perceive a higher reality in some way depends on her inability to see clearly. In a passage that has already been quoted, the narrator tells the reader, in tones of complete approbation, that

She was blind, you see, to many things obvious to others – likely to tread in the wrong places, as Celia had warned her; yet her blindness to whatever did not lie in her own pure purpose carried her safely by the side of precipices where vision would have been perilous with fear. (p. 408)

The dangers of 'precipices' here provide a gloss on an earlier description of Dorothea's hopes: 'The clear heights where she expected to walk in full communion had become difficult to see even in her imagination' (p. 307). Lydgate is also associated with the imagery of heights and vision. When he found himself besotted with Laure, he reflected,

He had two selves within him apparently, and they must learn to accommodate each other and bear reciprocal impediments. Strange, that some of us, with quick alternate vision, see beyond our infatuations, and even while we rave on the heights, behold the wide plain where our persistent self pauses and awaits us. (p. 182)

But Lydgate's ability to see both far and near does not help him. It merely confirms the disastrous split that he allows to exist between his vocation and his domestic preferences.

Blindness, myopia, awakening, enlightenment and vision: these concepts form a mounting pattern of images that structure much of

Dorothea's spiritual experience in the novel. She seeks a 'lamp' and finds it, not in Casaubon's knowledge, but in Ladislaw's 'radiance' and in the everyday light of the mundane world, which she comes to appreciate after her prolonged ordeal of night-watches with Casaubon and later, on her own. This imagery also links Dorothea with the pier-glass image of Chapter 27. In that extended 'parable', the ego is likened to a candle (perhaps the taper with which Casaubon approaches his discoveries), which distorts all external circumstances so that they appear to reflect the subject. The image of the seemingly concentric circles of scratches congregating around the light is superimposed on the image of the 'pier-glass' or mirror, to provide a double metaphor of egoism, through images of light, narcissism, knowledge and limitation. Dorothea early comes to appreciate that Casaubon 'had an equivalent centre of self, whence the lights and shadows must always fall with a certain difference' (p. 243). Interpretation of external events comes from a subjective perspective. In addition, the individual is reflected in the eyes of others, so that their opinions and reactions bounce back versions of the subject, sometimes flattering, sometimes distinctly unflattering. David Daiches summarizes the idea behind this imagery, when he says, 'do we use other people as mirrors in which to see ourselves, or do we use circumstances as windows through which to look – really to look – at others?'.

Perhaps the most explicit statement of this idea in the novel is in Fred Vincy's realization of the difference between his own view of himself and others' perspectives on him and his role in events, when he confesses to the Garths that he has not redeemed the debt which Caleb Garth has underwritten. We are told, 'his pain in the affair beforehand had consisted almost entirely in the sense that he must seem dishonourable, and sink in the opinion of the Garths' (p. 281) – this is a subjective and an egoistic concern for how he 'looks', for his own 'image'. 'But at this moment he suddenly saw himself as a pitiful rascal who was robbing two women of their savings' (p. 281). Neither version is totally true, but the change in Fred's perspective is from seeing matters through his eyes to seeing them through the equally subjective eyes of others. It is unflattering but salutary for Fred.

This notion is explored in varying ways through the experiences of other characters. Public opinion and rumour, so powerful in the novel, can reflect an individual in brutally honest, and even distorting, ways. Mr Vincy succumbs to the temptation of telling Bulstrode his opinion of him: '"You like to be master, there's no denying that; you must be first chop in heaven, else you won't like it much"' (p. 159), and

Bulstrode finds himself 'seeing a very unsatisfactory reflection of himself in the coarse unflattering mirror which that manufacturer's mind presented to the subtler lights and shadows of his fellow-men' (p. 159). Following a list of various uncomplimentary reactions to Casaubon, a general authorial comment emphasizes the necessary distortions of others' subjective views:

I am not sure that the greatest man of his age, if ever that solitary superlative existed, could escape these unfavourable reflections of himself in various small mirrors; and even Milton, looking for his portrait in a spoon, must submit to have the facial angle of a bumpkin. (p. 110)

Amid honest, unflattering, and even inaccurate reflections, the notion of a single 'truth' evaporates, and only versions of a person remain, each with conflicting grounds for substantiation. Seeing, and looking, become active modes of approaching the external world, always through the prism of one's subjectivity. As Hillis Miller says,

Seeing . . . is for Eliot not a neutral, objective, dispassionate or passive act. It is the creative projection of light from an egotistic center (sic) motivated by desire and need.[10]

Vision, like sympathy, is one of the narrator's many attributes. *Middlemarch* may be a novel *about* limited points of view, but the narrator has the ability to see microscopically, at the level of the day-to-day, and from an overseeing perspective. Correspondingly, the 'I' of the narrator, while certainly not shy in the text, possesses no personality and therefore little subjectivity. Comments are confined to, for example, generalizing expressions of sympathy with a human condition, as in the case of Casaubon:

For my part I am very sorry for him. It is an uneasy lot at best, to be what we call highly taught and yet not to enjoy: to be present at this great spectacle of life and never to be liberated from a small hungry shivering self . . . Doubtless some ancient Greek has observed that behind the big mask and the speaking-trumpet, there must always be our poor little eyes peeping as usual and our timorous lips more or less under anxious control. (p. 314)

The constant movement of the narrator from near to far, and back again, produces a sensation of vertigo when we read:

If we had a keen vision and feeling of all ordinary human life, it would be like hearing the grass grow and the squirrel's heart beat, and we should die of that roar which lies on the other side of silence. As it is, the quickest of us walk about well wadded with stupidity. (p. 226)

Metaphors proliferate here. The narrator tells us what a 'keen vision' would be like by using the images of hearing 'the grass grow and the squirrel's heart beat'. Yet at the same time, such vision is impossible and undesirable. The 'quickest of us' enjoy 'stupidity'. Simultaneously, the narrator has offered us the 'vision' and stated its inaccessibility.

Imagery, simile and metaphor provide meaning by substituting one thing for another or by likening one thing to another: they therefore push towards meaning while constantly displacing it on to another field of reference. This occurs outstandingly in the case of the central image in *Middlemarch*, that of the web. The book itself is like a web, with strands interweaving to produce a texture, hence also, a text. The narrator tells us explicitly that

I at least have so much to do in unravelling certain human lots, and seeing how they were woven and interwoven, that all the light I can command must be concentrated on this particular web, and not dispersed over that tempting range of relevancies called the universe. (p. 170)

And in this 'Study of Provincial Life', which aims to be both microscopic and conceptual, the methodology owes a great deal to the similar visual image of the grid, placed over a community to produce a patterning of interrelationships that can be understood. The narrator moves from one nexus of the web, or grid, to another, to observe the profound effects of one part of the social fabric on another, as when she says, 'In watching effects, if only of an electric battery, it is often necessary to change our place and examine a particular mixture or group at some distance from the point where the movement we are interested in was set up' (p. 434) – in this case referring to the way that Brooke's encounter with Dagley has led to Caleb Garth's good fortune.

Therefore, the image of the web reinforces the organic and social identity of *Middlemarch*. Within that web, each individual has a role and place. But the metaphor allows it to be seen that a web can also be a kind of trap, and images of enmeshment abound. Characters spin their own webs of social interaction by living in a community, by marrying and becoming a part of a society that once did not know them: this happens particularly to Lydgate, and Bulstrode too is eventually forced to recognize the degree of his membership in Middlemarch life. Lydgate boasts to Farebrother that he has chosen Middlemarch rather than London in order to be able to proceed with his work without interference or distraction:

'In the country, people have less pretension to knowledge, and are less of companions, but for that reason they affect one's *amour-propre* less: one makes less bad blood, and can follow one's own course more quietly.' (p. 204)

Farebrother gently corrects Lydgate's condescending attitude by saying, '"we Middlemarchers are not so tame as you take us to be. We have our intrigues and our parties"' (p. 205). There immediately follows Lydgate's dilemma over whom to vote for in the election of a chaplain for the fever hospital. Lydgate would like to vote for Farebrother, but needs Bulstrode's support for his own ambitions, and Bulstrode's man is Tyke. 'For the first time Lydgate was feeling the hampering threadlike pressure of small social conditions, and their frustrating complexity' (p. 210). He is drawn further and further into the life of the town, for with each attachment he forms, he creates ties, loyalties and obligations. Mrs Bulstrode hints to Lydgate that he is compromising Rosamond's prospects of marriage with other young men, and his initial response is that Rosamond has been as light-hearted as he 'but the people she lived among were blunderers and busybodies' (p. 333). Yet those hints act as a mental web: 'momentary speculations as to all the possible grounds for Mrs Bulstrode's hints had managed to get woven like slight clinging hairs into the more substantial web of his thoughts' (pp. 334–5), and Lydgate is imperceptibly but surely prepared for engagement: 'he left the house an engaged man, whose soul was not his own, but the woman's to whom he had bound himself' (p. 336). The threads of the web should remind us of the predatory function of a spider's web here, binding victims fast.

Bulstrode appropriates the image for his own use, as he does with so many things, when he says: '"it is not an easy thing even to thread a path for principles in the intricacies of the world – still less to make the thread clear for the careless and the scoffing"' (p. 158) to Mr Vincy. Here the web has become a labyrinth, and the notion of 'threading a path' serves to remind the reader of the myth of the Minotaur, already referred to when used by Ladislaw. In the myth, Ariadne helped Theseus to find his way through the labyrinth and slay the Minotaur, a monster which devoured sacrifices of the young. She helped him by giving him a ball of wool, with which to trace his way back following the thread. Bulstrode sees his role as a saviour, then. And the misappropriation of analogy multiplies when we recall that Rosamond casts herself as Ariadne when Lydgate stays away for ten days: 'Poor Rosamond lost her appetite and felt as forlorn as Ariadne – as a charming stage Ariadne left behind with all her boxes full of costumes and no hope of a coach' (p. 334). The specific reference here is to the fact that Theseus later deserted Ariadne, leaving her on the island of Naxos, and Rosamond figures her sense of desertion in these terms, extremely self-consciously and without losing her decorum. Yet underlying this is the irony that while Ariadne released Theseus from the labyrinth, Rosamond is entrapping Lydgate in a labyrinth of their joint making.

Gillian Beer observes that the image of the web exists not only as a spatial metaphor but also as a metaphor for the enmeshment of the individual in time, past, present and future. Bulstrode finds himself overtaken by his past, and significantly unable to look out of a window, but able only to see a reflection of the room behind him: his past, on which he has turned his back. The scene in Chapter 71 where Bulstrode is accused and condemned by fellow members of the Board shows his necessary entanglement in the 'petty medium' or web of Middlemarch, and when Lydgate helps the collapsing Bulstrode from the room, the notions of support, compromise and guilt by association are linked together: Lydgate is implicated in Bulstrode's disgrace by having accepted money from him while attending Raffles. Both these outsiders have been brought down by their disregard for the demands of social life.

Lydgate, whose research, as has been seen, resembles George Eliot's narrative project, fails to link the insights he gains to any personal experience. The description of Bichat's discoveries informs us of Lydgate's search for a 'common basis'. Significantly, the notion of the web recurs:

That great Frenchman first carried out the conception that living bodies, fundamentally considered, are not associations of organs which can be understood by studying them first apart, and then as it were federally; but must be regarded as consisting of certain primary webs or tissues, out of which the various organs – brain, heart, lungs, and so on – are compacted, as the various accommodations of a house are built up in various proportions of wood, iron, stone, brick, zinc, and the rest, each material having its peculiar composition and proportions. No man, one sees, can understand and estimate the entire structure or its parts – what are its frailties and what its repairs, without knowing the nature of the materials. (p. 177)

The point of this technical description is that there is no independence of the elements of an organic or social structure: one must come to know the 'primary webs or tissues' from which everything springs. Therefore, commonality – the medium of Middlemarch, the social fabric – is more important than the difference of individual members. Lydgate's reading of Bichat is used in the text to link Lydgate's scientific research to the poetic metaphors of the web.

While the similarities between human beings are more telling than their differences, so this passage suggests, the social fabric remains an ambiguous presence, its ambiguity conveyed powerfully by the shifting and working of metaphor. As a young girl, Dorothea finds herself, as she sees it, 'hemmed in by a social life which seemed nothing but a labyrinth of petty courses, a walled-in maze of small paths that led no whither' (p. 51). Tess Cosslett argues, however, that 'threads' and 'chains' are linked with 'channels' and 'currents', and that therefore the web operates in the following way:

those who do not accept its limitations find themselves struggling against a restrictive binding force; those who accept their bonds find opportunities for sympathetic expansion and effective action as parts in the social organism.

The threads of the web can become pathways of action through which the individual can escape the ego and move towards others. Ultimately, the image of the web comes to resemble an image of irrigation implicit in the equally ambiguous closing description of Dorothea: 'Her full nature ... spent itself in channels which had no great name on the earth. But the effect of her being on those around her was incalculably diffusive' (p. 896).

5. Science and the Novel

In the texture of allusions that makes up *Middlemarch*, references to science are as powerful and numerous as those to literature, myth or history. Michael Mason comments on how 'scientific language is appropriated for the novel's expression',[11] and in *Darwin's Plots* Gillian Beer reminds her readers that language 'that has now lost its scientific bearing still bore a freight of controversy and assertion for George Eliot and her first readers'; indeed, *Middlemarch* struck early readers as being laden with scientific vocabulary. In the course of earlier discussion in this study of *Middlemarch*, the scientific allusions have been mentioned frequently. The purpose of this section is to summarize their range and to discuss some examples in detail.

It is evident that one of the roles that the author assumes is that of scientist. She proposes a 'Study' of provincial life; in her tracing of causes and trains of events she moves from one area of investigation to another, employing the metaphor of the microscope. In the opening sentence of the Prelude, she links time and science by using the word 'experiment': 'the history of man, and how the mysterious mixture behaves under the varying experiments of Time' (p. 25). Here, 'man' is subjected to the active workings of a personified notion of 'time' – through the passage of time, his 'history' develops and changes. It is a curious way of beginning a novel, and it works to propose an ambitious enterprise. The slow effects are evolutionary ones, and the author will provide a shaping intelligence through which to interpret the results of Time's experiments.

The habitual recourse to scientific vocabulary generally shows the way that *Middlemarch* is an up-to-date novel of the late 1860s. Frequently the imagery used was in circulation at the time, whereas now it may merely strike the reader as complex and sometimes rather odd in analogy. A simple example is a reference to 'Lord Megatherium' in Chapter 6. This should remind the reader of Darwin's discovery of the fossilized skeleton of the extinct species, Megatherium, or giant sloth, at Punta Alta. The reference in full is a description of Mrs Cadwallader:

All the more did the affairs of the great world interest her, when communicated in the letters of high-born relations: the way in which fascinating younger sons had gone to the dogs by marrying their mistresses; the fine old-blooded idiocy of young Lord Tapir, and the furious gouty humours of old Lord Megatherium; (p. 83)

It is a rather flippant reference, yet it expands to imply the outdated world of Mrs Cadwallader's aristocratic connections, the ironically styled 'great world' – soon to become, like Megatherium, extinct.

George Eliot uses scientific language with fluency and ease. Passages of commentary often slide from references to literature or history to science and the natural world almost imperceptibly. Mr Brooke's inconsistency in hoping that Casaubon will be given a deanery when he is later to deliver a radical speech condemning the income of bishops is the occasion of an authorial meditation on the ironies wrought by the passage of time, and on history, yet it modulates into a metaphor about mining coal:

What elegant historian would neglect a striking opportunity for pointing out that his heroes did not foresee the history of the world, or even their own actions? – For example, that Henry of Navarre, when a Protestant baby, little thought of being a Catholic monarch; or that Alfred the Great, when he measured his laborious nights with burning candles, had no idea of future gentlemen measuring their idle days with watches. Here is a mine of truth, which, however vigorously it may be worked, is likely to outlast our coal. (pp. 90–1)

In a similar way, the scene in which Lydgate falls in love with Rosamond shifts in language through a number of different areas:

That moment of naturalness was the crystallizing feather-touch: it shook flirtation into love . . . an idea had thrilled through the recesses within him which had a miraculous effect in raising the power of passionate love lying buried there in no sealed sepulchre, but under the lightest, easily pierced mould. (p. 335)

At first, love is 'resurrected' in terms that evoke religious notions: 'miraculous', and 'sealed sepulchre'. The metaphor then changes to become reminiscent of plants pushing new shoots up through the 'mould', meaning here the earth. The earlier use of the adjective 'crystallizing' also carries with it overtones of a process in science.

This fluency enables George Eliot at times to allude to the controversies of the 1860s merely by using a certain discourse. Chapter 35 begins with a playful discussion about the animals entering the Ark:

one may imagine that allied species made much private remark on each other, and were tempted to think that so many forms feeding on the same store of fodder were eminently superfluous, as tending to diminish the rations. (I fear the part played by the vultures on that occasion would be too painful for art to represent, those birds being disadvantageously naked about the gullet, and apparently without rites and ceremonies.) (p. 365)

This is primarily an analogy with the mourners at Featherstone's funeral, who all want to receive as much of his estate as possible. The description also identifies human greed as animalistic, thus raising questions about human nature. It refers to the Biblical story only to substitute notions drawn from evolutionary theory about conflict and struggle in the animal world.

It has already been noted that images from biology, geology and zoology recur in descriptions of the changing relationship between Lydgate and Rosamond. Their slowly developing incompatibility, their disagreements like conflicts between creatures from different species, Rosamond's predatory power and her eventual survival as the 'fittest', are all striking because of the way in which they are described. Sometimes the metaphors being used are extended into thematic points. Many readers have noted the moment when Lydgate barters with Farebrother, offering him Brown's *Microscopic Observations on the Pollen of Plants* (1828) in exchange for a 'lovely anencephalous monster' (p. 202). This specimen of a creature without a brain fascinates Lydgate, who significantly calls it 'lovely'. If we are feeling particularly critical of Rosamond, the parallel between her and the monster is not hard to detect: Lydgate is seduced by appearances and by a fleeting fascination, and is ready to pay with his scientific library.

Rosamond is not only seen in terms of a number of predatory creatures, but she is also posed against her environment, Middlemarch. 'She was admitted to be the flower of Mrs Lemon's school, the chief school in the county' (p. 123), and as such is a perfect product of her environment. When she plays the piano for Lydgate,

A hidden soul seemed to be flowing forth from Rosamond's fingers; and so indeed it was, since souls live on in perpetual echoes, and to all fine expression there goes somewhere an originating activity, if it be only that of an interpreter. Lydgate was taken possession of, and began to believe in her as something exceptional. After all, he thought, one need not be surprised to find the rare conjunctions of nature under circumstances apparently unfavourable: come where they may, they always depend on conditions that are not obvious. (p. 190)

Lydgate is unprepared to find such skill in the provinces. He attempts to explain it to himself in terms of evolutionary theory, but he also thinks of her as 'exceptional'. His interpretation is misconceived, for Rosamond has merely mimicked her genuinely exceptional tutor; she herself is a typical product of the provinces, in more senses than one.

Middlemarch as environment becomes Middlemarch a threatening predator itself in such phrases as the one which tells us that the town 'counted on swallowing Lydgate and assimilating him very comfortably' (p. 183). Not only can human nature be accurately described in language from biology and zoology, but provincial life, here, is an engorging presence or land-mass. This indirectly lets us know how George Eliot wants us to think of the town, the community and the characteristic ways of thought.

Perhaps it is fitting that many of the images appear to cluster around Lydgate in particular, for as a character he brings science into the thematic concerns of the novel. Even though his research into the 'primitive tissue' is slightly misdirected, 'not quite in the way required by the awaiting answer' (p. 178), and even though he fails in his aspirations to reform medical knowledge, he brings to his work an imaginative and shaping intelligence:

that delightful labour of the imagination which is not mere arbitrariness, but the exercise of disciplined power – combining and constructing with the clearest eye for probabilities and the fullest obedience to knowledge; and then, in yet more energetic alliance with impartial Nature, standing aloof to invent tests by which to try its own work. (pp. 193–4)

This describes an active participation in the gaining of knowledge, where the imagination combines and constructs hypotheses in the light of what is already known, and where results are tested over again to confirm that the imagination has worked alongside nature. The experimental method is further described a few sentences later:

he was enamoured of that arduous invention which is the very eye of research, provisionally framing its object and correcting it to more and more exactness of relation. (p. 194)

Lydgate's procedure is explained meticulously because other researchers in the novel lack his talents and his insight. Casaubon superficially resembles Lydgate in the fact that both men seek a point of origin: Casaubon the 'Key to All Mythologies', Lydgate the 'common basis'. But Casaubon has remained stranded at a point in his work where he has merely collected and begun to tabulate his findings. He lacks the ability and power to 'frame his object', he lacks 'that arduous invention which is the very eye of research'. More than his egoism, his insecurity, or his aridity of topic, it is this absence of 'that delightful labour of the imagination', 'that arduous invention', that consigns Casaubon's work to failure. On the other hand, Farebrother represents a different school

139

of science. He, unlike Casaubon, is not unequal to his task but he has conceived differently of his task from Lydgate. He says, '"I fancy I have made an exhaustive study of the entomology of this district. I am going on both with the fauna and flora; but I have at least done my insects well"' (p. 202). He observes and collects natural specimens, and is interested in classifying new species. His study contains 'insects ranged in fine gradation, with names subscribed in exquisite writing' (p. 204). Farebrother does not include in his scientific role that fusion of nature, intellect and imagination that so fires Lydgate.

Lydgate's wide-ranging methodology is important because of the parallel with George Eliot's own aims in *Middlemarch*. It is also important because it links him, through the exercise of imagination, with Dorothea's quite unscientific, but sympathetic, identification with the world around her. She responds to people and their situations with a lively interest and imaginative feeling. This is evident in her friendship with Farebrother, her affection for Ladislaw, but most significantly in her championing of Lydgate when he suffers private unhappiness and public disgrace. Dorothea's access to knowledge is in contrast to Casaubon's sterile accumulation of facts, and runs in tandem with Lydgate's aspiring research. In the end, it is imaginative sympathy that must prevail over other roads to knowledge, and that does prevail over limited definitions of science that emphasize observation and tabulation. In a novel that expresses through its language an engagement with 'science', then, science becomes a term that is questioned and redefined.

6. The Authorial Voice

If you want to know more particularly how Mary looked, ten to one you will see a face like hers in the crowded street tomorrow, if you are there on the watch: she will not be among those daughters of Zion who are haughty, and walk with stretched-out necks and wanton eyes, mincing as they go: let all those pass, and fix your eyes on some small plump brownish person of firm but quiet carriage, who looks about her, but does not suppose that anybody is looking at her. If she has a broad face and square brow, well-marked eyebrows and curly dark hair, a certain expression of amusement in her glance which her mouth keeps the secret of, and for the rest features entirely insignificant – take that ordinary but not disagreeable person for a portrait of Mary Garth. If you made her smile she would show you perfect little teeth; if you made her angry, she would not raise her voice, but would probably say one of the bitterest things you have ever tasted the flavour of; if you did her a kindness, she would never forget it. (pp. 442–3)

To many readers, the authorial voice is the most noticeable presence in *Middlemarch*. This passage of characterization and description demonstrates many of the features of the authorial voice that the reader notes. It addresses the reader directly: 'If you want to know . . .' It casts a sketch of Mary in terms of generalized observation about a whole class and type of person: 'some small plump brownish person of firm but quiet carriage . . .' It is confident of a shared set of values with the reader, and it employs a highly sophisticated and allusive language: 'she will not be among those daughters of Zion who are haughty'. In the series of hypotheses, the voice claims knowledge about human nature and behaviour. It is a sympathetic and humane voice, yet it is impersonal in its manner. We have already seen how this voice controls and directs action, and how it offers judgement and interpretation. Within a number of roles – scientist, humanist, historian, moralist – it displays confidence, erudition and omniscience.

A constant modulation from the particular to the general is evident in *Middlemarch*. The reactions of characters are set in a context of common human feeling and human nature. When Lydgate has taken the disgraced Bulstrode home, he finds that he cannot face going home himself, because he feels so bitter and resentful about his lot that he is afraid he would be cruel to Rosamond. We are told that 'he was very miserable' (p. 793). This then moves into an authoritative generalization:

Only those who know the supremacy of the intellectual life – the life which has a seed of ennobling thought and purpose within it – can understand the grief of one who falls from that serene activity into the absorbing soul-wasting struggle with worldly annoyances. (p. 793)

The narrator here teaches the reader how to understand the complexities of Lydgate's feelings, which involves an understanding of 'the supremacy of the intellectual life'. We always see the feelings and situations of the characters within this larger framework. There is a corresponding confidence about what is going on within the character's mind. Lydgate is not just 'miserable', he is going through a 'grief' of falling from his intellectual aspirations to the tribulations of social existence.

In another example, Casaubon's confrontation with the possible imminence of his own death is an occasion for the narrator to describe human reactions in general:

Here was a man who now for the first time found himself looking into the eyes of death – who was passing through one of those rare moments of experience when we feel the truth of a commonplace, which is as different from what we call knowing it, as the vision of waters upon the earth is different from the delirious vision of the water which cannot be had to cool the burning tongue. When the commonplace 'We must all die' transforms itself suddenly into the acute consciousness 'I must die – and soon', then death grapples us, and his fingers are cruel; afterwards, he may come to fold us in his arms as our mother did, and our last moment of dim earthly discerning may be like the first. To Mr Casaubon now, it was as if he suddenly found himself on the dark river-brink and heard the plash of the oncoming oar, not discerning the forms, but expecting the summons. (pp. 461–2)

A narrator who undertakes to describe the sensations of facing one's own death must either be very wise or more knowing than the majority of mere mortals. George Eliot's authorial voice partakes of both wisdom and superhuman perception. This passage also demonstrates the narrator's habit of drawing the reader into involvement with the characters: 'when we feel the truth of a commonplace', 'death grapples us'. It relies heavily on metaphoric and allusive language. There is the pervasive use of water imagery, working here to emphasize 'the truth of a commonplace', and Casaubon's own feelings are given echoes of Charon, the boatman ferrying souls across the river Acheron in classical mythology: 'heard the plash of the oncoming oar'.

In the world of the authorial voice, there is an explanation for (almost) everything. 'What happens' is accessible to the narrator, and so we follow her, having been made aware of the circumstances and general truths of events. This creates a constant presence of irony in the text, where the author and the reader share a knowledge about what is happening when the character often does not. It is a technique that allows for tremendous perspective and for an overview that individual characters would not often be able to articulate. When Ladislaw tells Dorothea that he intends to leave Middlemarch soon, in Chapter 54, the narrator glosses Dorothea's grief:

She did not know then that it was Love who had come to her briefly as in a dream before awaking, with the hues of morning on his wings – that it was Love to whom she was sobbing her farewell as his image was banished by the blameless rigour of irresistible day. She only felt that there was something irrevocably amiss and lost in her lot . . . (p. 592)

Here the narrator knows what Dorothea is feeling and knows what Dorothea does not know yet. Dramatic irony is present in a more painful form at the moment when Mrs Bulstrode, beset by suspicions of her husband's disgrace, finally reaches her brother's office:

he rose from his seat to meet her, took her by the hand, and said, with his impulsive rashness –
    'God help you, Harriet! you know all.'
    That moment was perhaps worse than any which came after. It contained that concentrated experience which in great crises of emotion reveals the bias of a nature, and is prophetic of the ultimate act which will end an intermediate struggle. Without that memory of Raffles she might still have thought only of monetary ruin, but now along with her brother's look and words there darted into her mind the idea of some guilt in her husband – then, under the working of terror came the image of her husband exposed to disgrace – and then, after an instant of scorching shame in which she felt only the eyes of the world, with one leap of her heart she was at his side in mournful but unreproaching fellowship with shame and isolation. All this went on within her in a mere flash of time . . . (pp. 805–6)

When Mr Vincy says, '"you know all"', Mrs Bulstrode does not, and we register this dramatic irony. The irony is doubled when we learn that this comment is what reveals to her the gravity of the situation – it makes her know. The authorial voice then proceeds to inform us that this moment is the absolute turning-point in her perception, during which she surveys the present and future and opts for loyalty to her husband. There is no way in which Mrs Bulstrode as a character could express to herself or to anyone else the sensations of this moment. It is the narrator who is in firm control of knowledge about the situation, the moment of choice, and Mrs Bulstrode's feelings. She gives the reader the knowledge to register this example of character in process.

Some readers of *Middlemarch* feel oppressed by such dominance. The authorial voice will not leave matters, or the reader, alone. Arnold Kettle talks of 'a certain forcing of the issue, one might call it, a tendency to illustrate a shade too often the moral generalization'. But he also adds that the voice's insistence 'that we should continually relate her fiction to our lives' is 'one of the great strengths of George Eliot as a novelist'. Such mingled irritation and admiration is a common reaction. Consequently, the prominence of the authorial voice has given rise to a great deal of critical analysis. *Middlemarch* is often cited as a representative text of 'classic realism', in which the authorial voice dominates all the other voices and discourses in the novel. That domination has already been shown, in the way that points of action, interaction or confrontation are followed (and often preceded, too) by generalization or exegesis. In addition, the authorial voice, by claiming knowledge, tends to function 'simply as a window on reality'.[12] Its language is 'transparent', in the sense that it assumes that it is expressing some reality in the world. Thus, characters' feelings and reactions are always related to some general trait in human nature. There are no aberrant, inexplicable emotions present in the novel. If they appear to be so, the authorial voice is there at the reader's shoulder, making clear the logic and humanity underlying the apparently unexpected.

This analysis of the authorial voice in *Middlemarch* as an exemplar of 'classic realism' functions as a means of pointing out the normalizing project of much nineteenth-century fiction, in which certain 'truths' about human nature are confirmed, creating an ideological strait-jacket. Certainly the voice's power and authority convey security. Yet the textuality of the novel, shown in extended discussions earlier of the historical, literary and scientific allusions present everywhere in the language of the novel, reflects an uncertainty about the absoluteness of any one kind of knowledge, and an awareness of the historical relativity of knowledge. This must also be borne in mind when we consider the narrator and the authorial voice. Penny Boumelha touches on this when she says,

We are dealing, then, less with some objective chronicle of truth than with an incomplete, positioned and contradictory account that in any case draws on saints' lives, fairy-tale and legend as well as on the conventions of mimetic realism.[13]

However, while there is simultaneously a pressure towards a homogeneous version of 'truth', and a betraying uncertainty, there still remains that recognizable *voice*, speaking to the reader about a stunning range of topics. Who is speaking? Even when the narrator occasionally refers to herself in the first person, she remains impersonal, almost anonymous. It is possible to describe various features of the voice, and even to characterize it to some extent, but it remains elusive. In *The Country and the City*, Raymond Williams focuses on the implications of the narrator's grasp and articulation of matters. He identifies a disjunction between the community that George Eliot chooses to portray and her own educated access, unavailable to her subjects, to understanding and means of expression. There is another gap, too: that between her subjects, who lack sophisticated means of thinking about themselves, and her audience, who are assumed to be capable of following her highly articulate range of style. Ordinary people in George Eliot's novels tend to be relegated to a dialect in their speech. This distances and demotes them, so that they become a kind of representative chorus, rather than individuals. This is evident in the case of Timothy Cooper's brief but memorable speech to Caleb Garth, resisting the notion that progress will benefit the labouring man. The text contains this, as we have seen, through commentary and ironic restatement, yet it hangs there as an admission that some kinds of experience cannot be incorporated by the authorial voice, or by the ideology that pervades the novel. In the case of characters given the power of received pronunciation and – closely connected – more introspection, there is still a distance between the character's understanding and the author's, a distance filled (perhaps inevitably filled) with irony.

A final example should demonstrate these contradictions and problems. Bulstrode is forced to make a decision that he will be responsible for, after hours of searching his conscience and of prayer:

Before he had quite undressed, Mrs Abel rapped at the door; he opened it an inch, so that he could hear her speak low.

'If you please, sir, should I have no brandy nor nothing to give the poor creetur? He feels sinking away, and nothing else will he swaller – and but little strength in it, if he did – only the opium. And he says more and more he's sinking down through the earth.'

To her surprise, Mr Bulstrode did not answer. A struggle was going on within him.

'I think he must die for want o' support, if he goes on in that way. When I nursed my poor master, Mr Robisson, I had to give him port-wine and brandy constant, and a big glass at a time,' added Mrs Abel with a touch of remonstrance in her tone.

But again Mr Bulstrode did not answer immediately, and she continued, 'It's not a time to spare when people are at death's door, nor would you wish it, sir, I'm sure. Else I should give him our own bottle o' rum as we keep by us. But a sitter-up so as you've been, and doing everything as laid in your power –'

Here a key was thrust through the inch of doorway, and Mr Bulstrode said huskily, 'That is the key of the wine-cooler. You will find plenty of brandy there.'

Early in the morning – about six – Mr Bulstrode rose and spent some time in prayer. Does any one suppose that private prayer is necessarily candid – necessarily goes to the roots of action! Private prayer is inaudible speech, and speech is representative: who can represent himself just as he is, even in his own reflections? Bulstrode had not yet unravelled in his thought the confused promptings of the last four-and-twenty hours. (p. 763)

We are not shown this moment of temptation from Bulstrode's point of view. His silence, and the huskiness of his voice when he finally succumbs, are sufficient to indicate the crisis he is undergoing. Mrs Abel's powers of innocent persuasion are relayed in a muted dialect, which serves to underline her ignorance and lack of power. After a break of some hours in the action, the authorial voice resumes a narrative, and generalizes about the honesty of prayer. Bulstrode is ignorant of what he thinks or feels about what has happened. His confusion is contained by the authorial voice, who is confident that she, and the reader, know how to interpret events. Sympathy with characters goes hand in hand with a superior moral knowledge. It is a superiority that the reader cannot escape, unless that escape be through the range of discourses in the novel.

7. Feminism and the Novel

With the development of feminist literary criticism in the 1970s and 1980s, George Eliot has become a focus of attention in a relatively new way. In what ways may her writing practice and her novels be described as 'feminist' in intention and effect? To what degree was she a feminist, or rather, a supporter of the burgeoning women's movement that was so active, especially in the 1840s, 1850s and 1860s?

These are not idle questions, for George Eliot's life leads us to contemplate her as a rebel: rejecting her father's authority and established religion, earning her living by journalism, and later, fiction, as few women of her period could or did, studying seriously, living openly with a married man, and finally marrying a man much younger than herself. All these instances indicate her desire for autonomy and authenticity. But in general, it seems that her iconoclasm in her private life was not reflected in the patterns of her fiction. Indeed, some readers feel that that iconoclasm was the cause of a deep conservatism in her writing. Conscious of the cost of what she had rejected or left behind in attaining an independent life, she glorified the past, her childhood scenes, and the traditional roles for women of wife and mother. One critic puts it wittily:

Feminist critics are angry with George Eliot because she did not permit Dorothea Brooke in 'Middlemarch' to do what George Eliot did in real life: translate, publish articles, edit a periodical, refuse to marry until she was middle-aged, live an independent existence as a spinster, and finally live openly with a man whom she could not marry.[14]

This point of view tends to conflate author and character, and lapses into prescriptiveness, but the puzzling mismatch between George Eliot's experiences and themes remains.

The characterization of Rosamond Vincy is an interesting point at which to begin. She is the epitome of the desirable and accomplished young lady. She

never showed any unbecoming knowledge, and was always that combination of correct sentiments, music, dancing, drawing, elegant note-writing, private album for extracted verse, and perfect blond loveliness, which made the irresistible woman for the doomed man of that date. (p. 301)

In everything that she does, she studiedly achieves femininity, until it becomes a role:

(Every nerve and muscle in Rosamond was adjusted to the consciousness that she was being looked at. She was by nature an actress of parts that entered into her *physique*: she even acted her own character, and so well, that she did not know it to be precisely her own.) (p. 144)

Although she is adept at those ladylike pursuits of needlework, music and horse-riding, then, the artificiality and the efforts involved in achieving this stereotype of femininity are shown in the portrayal of Rosamond. She is treated very harshly by George Eliot: at least, many readers have thought so. Henry James admired the characterization, calling Rosamond 'a rare psychological study', 'this veritably mulish domestic flower', who represents in his opinion 'the fatality of British decorum'. Significantly, (male) reviewers tended at times to feel protective towards Rosamond in the face of her author's treatment of her. Sidney Colvin, writing in *The Fortnightly Review*, asserted that towards Rosamond, George Eliot 'shows a really merciless animosity, and gibbets her as an example of how an unworthy wife may degrade the career of a man of high purposes and capacities'. R. H. Hutton, who wrote a series of reviews of the parts of *Middlemarch* as they came out, for the *Spectator*, objected at length when he had read Book III:

Celia Brooke and Rosamond Vincy are, to use an expressive, though rude, schoolboy phrase, 'always catching it' from the authoress, till we feel decidedly disposed to take their sides ... Take the following sentence, for instance, which we entirely object to, as quite beyond the proper duties of a painter of life, who has no right to try and rob her characters of the fair amount of sympathy which would be given to them in real life, except by making her picture more instructive and graphic than real life would ordinarily be. Rosamond is in love, and she has reason to fear that her castle-building has been a mistake: 'Poor Rosamond lost her appetite, and felt as forlorn as Ariadne – as a charming stage Ariadne left behind with all her boxes full of costumes and no hope of a coach.' Now, that is not an additional touch of the artist's; it is a malicious stab of the critic's, which makes us distrust our author's impartiality, and feel rather more disposed to take Rosamond's part than if the attack had not been made.

Gallant male responses apart, it is true that Rosamond becomes the occasion for a devastating critique on George Eliot's part of the social construction of femininity. Sir James Chettam, during his comically unsuccessful wooing of Dorothea, has delivered himself of the opinion that '"Every lady ought to be a perfect horsewoman, that she may accompany her husband"' (p. 44). Much later in the novel, Rosamond goes out riding, not to accompany Lydgate, but against his advice, and loses the baby that she is expecting. Sir James's criterion for a 'lady' ironically turns out to lead, not to docility, but to dissent, intransigence, and emotional failure. As Mrs Plymdale sourly notes, 'Rosamond had been educated to a ridiculous pitch, for what was the use of accomplishments which would be all laid aside as soon as she was married?' (p. 197). Rosamond's 'education' has been in feminine accomplishments that have the underlying purpose of attracting a man to marry, but they are unsuitable for the demands of marriage itself. An added irony is that, of course, Rosamond's education has, in another and important sense, been neglected. While Celia's blooming maternity signifies that she has successfully negotiated the passage from young lady to matron, Rosamond finds that her femininity and beguiling ways are useless to her once she is married, and force a destructive distance between her and her husband. For example, while in courtship, Lydgate feels that Rosamond's refusal to postpone the wedding at her father's demand shows a 'constancy of purpose' that was 'adorable' (p. 385), that same inflexibility and singleness of purpose within marriage frustrates him at every turn.

Yet it is possible to perceive the portrayal of Rosamond as sympathetic rather than punitive. Lydgate is just as responsible as Rosamond for their marital conflicts and disappointments. Rosamond is in part a victim of her time and place, just as Dorothea is, but in a different way. Rosamond has worked hard to become the perfect young lady that her society designates the most desirable role for young women. There is an implication that her egoism and inflexibility are results of an all too successful education in femininity. Significantly, she is not a 'failure' at the end of the novel. After Lydgate's early death, she 'married an elderly and wealthy physician, who took kindly to her four children. She made a very pretty show with her daughters, driving out in her carriage, and often spoke of her happiness as "a reward" – she did not say for what' (p. 893). There is irony in the fact of Rosamond's survival – she has proved, perhaps, 'fitter' than Lydgate in their mutual struggle – and also irony in her continuing egoism of regarding herself as deserving of 'a reward'. Yet the ironies do not completely mask the unhappiness that she *has* undergone with Lydgate, and the reader must concede that the picture of her in her carriage with her daughters is a confirmation of the ladylike existence that Rosamond was only ever educated for. Several critics take this sympathetic view of Rosamond. Kathleen Blake, for example, says:

In view of the doubtful pains it costs a woman to mark out anything more original, and in view of the odds against learning a taste for originality, or pains, at Miss Lemon's school, we are not invited to blame Rosamond with as much cold dislike as most critics permit themselves.[15]

There are some highly persuasive readings of *Middlemarch* which seek to define the extent of George Eliot's 'feminism' in the themes of the novel. The primary focus here is Dorothea: her aspirations, and the constraints placed upon her. The Prelude and Finale are both important for this discussion, as is the epigraph to Chapter 1:

> Since I can do no good because a woman,
> Reach constantly at something that is near it.
> *The Maid's Tragedy*: Beaumont and Fletcher

In the context of contemporaneous issues of women's education, the right to work, and legal rights, Dorothea's situation is compellingly relevant. Her ardour leads her to seek a role in life at the beginning of the novel: to seek a vocation, with all its connotations of both religious commitment and (gainful) occupation, as we have seen earlier. While Dorothea joins Lydgate, Ladislaw, Fred Vincy and others in the search for a vocation within the novel, her gender exacerbates the problem of vocation, so that her difficulties necessarily become bound up with the misfortunes of a woman's lot. In Chapter 1, she has already started an infant school in the village, and commenced 'plans' for village cottages; but:

For a long while she had been oppressed by the indefiniteness which hung in her mind, like a thick summer haze, over all her desire to make her life greatly effective. What could she do, what ought she to do? – she, hardly more than a budding woman, but yet with an active conscience and a great mental need, not to be satisfied by a girlish instruction comparable to the nibblings and judgements of a discursive mouse. (p. 50)

As she sympathetically observes of Ladislaw the first time that she meets him, and hears of his lack of direction, '"After all, people may really have in them some vocation which is not quite plain to themselves, may they not? They may seem idle and weak because they are growing"' (pp. 107–8). But her circumstances are less hopeful than Ladislaw's: she has had little formal education, merely a 'toy-box history of the world adapted to young ladies' (p. 112) and 'the shallows of ladies'-school literature' (p. 47). She is constrained by social expectations of what it is to be a young lady in her time and place, although unlike Rosamond she has never shown an aptitude for needlework, music or painting. 'What could she do, what ought she to do?' (p. 50) becomes a refrain in Dorothea's life, and the question is used, as we have seen, as a central motif in the lives of other female characters by the author.

Dorothea's yearning for an active and meaningful life is also thwarted by the narrow society in which she lives. She is 'hemmed in by a social life which seemed nothing' (p. 51). There is comedy in Dorothea's wilful disregard of the mundane and inflation of spiritual and intellectual goals that she has no means of defining adequately – often, the ridiculous collides with the sublime, as in her distressed reaction to the news that everyone expects her to marry Sir James Chettam: '"How can one ever do anything nobly Christian, living among people with such petty thoughts?"' (p. 60). But the comedy passes swiftly to poignancy: her striving to look beyond her immediate surroundings *is* a noble and embattled endeavour. Dorothea's solution, at this stage of the novel, and perhaps it is the only solution, is to identify marriage as the vehicle for 'an exalted enthusiasm about the ends of life' (p. 50). George Eliot makes her choice of Casaubon totally logical as, in her prosaic and limited social circle, Dorothea has no genuine standard against which to measure him. She therefore mistakes marriage for vocation and mistakes Casaubon for the teacher and sage who will provide her with the requisite education to 'understand' and thence to act. Once again, there is both comedy and poignancy in her disappointment at Lowick, before the marriage:

She felt some disappointment, of which she was yet ashamed, that there was nothing for her to do in Lowick; and in the next few minutes her mind had glanced over the possibility, which she would have preferred, of finding that her home would be in a parish which had a larger share of the world's misery, so that she might have had more active duties in it. Then, recurring to the future actually before her, she made a picture of more complete devotion to Mr Casaubon's aims, in which she would await new duties. Many such might reveal themselves to the higher knowledge gained by her in that companionship. (p. 103)

Although she comes perilously near to wishing for others' misery in order to gain an active role, we see here that she has already lost the possibility of being of some use in a wider sphere. In this passage, Dorothea dedicates herself even more seriously to marriage and to Casaubon. In the course of the novel, we see that dedication falter as it dawns on her that his scholarly endeavours are stagnant and out-of-date, and that he cannot offer her a pathway to enlightenment. As Mr Brooke has said, of marriage, '"It *is* a noose, you know. Temper, now. There is temper. And a husband likes to be master"' (p. 64).

Dorothea's mistakes are compounded of her ardour, her egoism, the milieu of Middlemarch, and, perhaps most importantly, the social role of women at the time. Male views of the nature and desirability of women abound, particularly in the early pages of the novel. We learn from commentators such as Brooke, Sir James and the guests at the dinner party in Chapter 10, that women are flighty, shallow-minded, and fit only to be seen on horseback or to be decorative. Dorothea does not gain approbation for her enthusiasm: Lydgate's initial reaction is to think, '"She is a good creature – that fine girl – but a little too earnest ... It is troublesome to talk to such women"' (p. 119). As George Eliot points out, Lydgate 'might possibly have experience before him which would modify his opinion as to the most excellent things in woman' (p. 120), but in general, such male preconceptions form the context for the lack of education extended to girls, and for the impossibility for a woman to be assertive. Throughout the novel, Dorothea is controlled in her actions by men. As Mrs Casaubon, she is bent to her husband's wishes and prejudices; as his widow, she is amusingly but firmly hectored by her brother-in-law, Sir James. She has no control over her property, even as a widow, for then it has been made subject to Casaubon's will. At the end of the novel, she says sadly to Celia, '"I never could do anything that I liked. I have never carried out any plan yet"' (p. 878). The only moments when a woman is allowed to make her own decision are when she is contemplating marriage, presumably because then, it is emotion (that quality associated with women above all) that is deemed to determine choice. Thus, she is not diverted from her unsuitable and unwise first marriage. And in her unplanned choice of a life with Ladislaw, she asserts herself only to renounce her financial independence and security. Her voice here, so plangent at the beginning of the novel, striking Ladislaw as being 'like the voice of a soul that had once lived in an Aeolian harp' (p. 105) when he first meets her, and so silenced throughout most of the novel, finally breaks through:

There was silence. Dorothea's heart was full of something that she wanted to say, and yet the words were too difficult. She was wholly possessed by them: at that moment debate was mute within her. And it was very hard that she could not say what she wanted to say ...

'Oh, I cannot bear it – my heart will break,' ... she said in a sobbing childlike way, 'We could live quite well on my own fortune – it is too much – seven hundred-a-year – I want so little – no new clothes – and I will learn what everything costs.' (p. 870)

This moment of assertiveness passes as she returns to marriage.

The 'Woman question' in *Middlemarch* was evident to early reviewers. Sidney Colvin identified it as being probably the primary intention of the author:

In her prelude and conclusion both, she seems to insist upon the design of illustrating the necessary disappointment of a woman's nobler aspirations in a society not made to second noble aspirations in a woman. And that is one of the most burning lessons which any writer could set themselves to illustrate.

He went on to debate the embodiment of the theme in Dorothea's story. In the *Spectator*, R. H. Hutton recognized the theme but voiced reservations:

If this was really George Eliot's drift, we do not think it particularly well worked out ... In fact the attempt of the 'prelude' and the final chapter to represent the book as an elaborate contribution to the 'Woman's' question, seems to us a mistake, meting out unjust measure to the entirely untrammelled imaginative power which the book displays.

The reviewer in *The Times* went one step further, and declined to believe that the topic was the central concern of the novel:

We do not think that this is at all intended, and if it be intended it is certainly not justified ... Her failures and mistakes are not due to the fact of her being a woman, but are simply those which belong to the common lot of human life.

It may be that while the treatment of Dorothea leans heavily on a discussion of women's rights and condition, it is not fully incorporated into the novel, being part of the original 'Miss Brooke' rather than a central theme of the finished *Middlemarch*.

Despite the demonstration that Dorothea's situation is partly caused by the situation pertaining to women at the time, there are elements that suggest a less radical analysis on the part of George Eliot. Dorothea's early identification of marriage as a channel for her vocation is pitiful, but nowhere is it suggested that she could thereafter find a different sphere for her energies. Florence Nightingale, on reading the novel in 1873, felt the lack of alternatives set forth in the book most strongly:

This author now can find no better outlet for the heroine ... *because* she cannot be a 'St Theresa' or an 'Antigone', than to marry an elderly sort of imposter ... Yet close at hand, in actual life ... was a woman ... and if we mistake not, a connection of the author's, who has managed to make her ideal very real indeed.

The woman to whom Florence Nightingale is referring was Octavia

Hill, the great reformer of housing for the poor in the second half of the nineteenth century, and influential figure in the founding of the National Trust. In 1865, her sister Gertrude had married G. H. Lewes's eldest son Charles. Florence Nightingale is partly right: Dorothea's false assumptions about what Casaubon can offer her merge into what seems like an authorial assumption that marriage *is*, in fact, the only vocation open to women. Dorothea's second marriage was among the most preliminary of George Eliot's notes for her story, and so it was always perceived as the fitting culmination of her development. One way of countering Florence Nightingale's criticism – and the feminist complaint quoted at the beginning of this section – is to observe that Dorothea is not intended by her author to be exceptional in her abilities. She may be unusual in her aspirations, but on the whole she is an example of the experiences of a whole section of the female population. As Arnold Kettle says, 'Dorothea is not Saint Theresa. She is an intelligent and sensitive girl born into the English landed ruling class of the early nineteenth century.'

Like so much of the characterization in *Middlemarch*, the portrayal of Dorothea is resistant to definition in its complexity. George Eliot certainly felt considerable ambivalence about the ending of Dorothea's story. The Finale discusses Dorothea's ultimate achievement. It originally appeared with some extra sentences in the penultimate paragraph. The second edition, published in 1874, upon which most modern texts are based, says:

Certainly those determining acts of her life were not ideally beautiful. They were the mixed result of a young and noble impulse struggling amidst the conditions of an imperfect social state, in which great feelings will often take the aspect of error, and great faith the aspect of illusion. (p. 896)

In the first edition, of 1871–2, this section ran:

Certainly those determining acts of her life were not ideally beautiful. They were the mixed result of young and noble impulse struggling under prosaic conditions. Among the many remarks passed on her mistakes, it was never said in the neighbourhood of Middlemarch that such mistakes could not have happened if the society into which she was born had not smiled on propositions of marriage from a sickly man to a girl less than half his own age – on modes of education which make a woman's knowledge another name for motley ignorance – on rules of conduct which are in flat contradiction with its own loudly-asserted beliefs. While this is the social air in which morals begin to breathe, there will be collisions such as those in Dorothea's life, where great feelings will often take the aspect of error, and great faith the aspect of illusion.

The reference to a society which 'smiled on propositions of marriage from a sickly man to a girl less than half his own age' is inaccurate, for the novel shows the amount of resistance to Dorothea's choice of Casaubon, in Celia, Mrs Cadwallader, Sir James, and even Mr Brooke. (On the other hand, Mr Cadwallader's attitude of detachment prevails.) Yet in the condemnation of a society that offers 'modes of education which make a woman's knowledge another name for motley ignorance', the Finale emphasizes how greatly the disadvantages of women's situations have affected Dorothea's life. In the absence of these sentences, the 1874 edition tends to convey a notion of Dorothea's ultimate fulfilment. Emotional contentment, it seems, is located in the marital bond. There are two conflicting aims for Dorothea: the accomplishment of some 'greatly effective' life in a public sphere, and the joy of emotional fulfilment in an exclusive relationship. The proposition in the Finale is that these cannot be combined in a totally satisfactory manner, at least for a woman:

No life would have been possible to Dorothea which was not filled with emotion, and she had now a life filled also with a beneficent activity which she had not the doubtful pains of discovering and marking out for herself. Will became an ardent public man ... Many who knew her, thought it a pity that so substantive and rare a creature should have been absorbed into the life of another, and be only known in a certain circle as a wife and mother. But no one stated exactly what else that was in her power she ought rather to have done. (p. 894)

The words, 'that was in her power', once again shift the focus of argument from a general picture of circumscribed ambition to a specific analysis of the conditions determining Dorothea's experience.

Among critics, there are some extreme responses to this ending. Kate Millet, in characteristically blunt language, says, 'She marries Will Ladislaw and can expect no more of life than the discovery of a good companion whom she can serve as a secretary.'[16] This observation does alert us to the fact that Dorothea has found in Ladislaw some of the powers that she thought she saw in Casaubon: the dedication to a worthy cause, the appreciation of a helpmate. Kathleen Blake, and others, argue that Ladislaw is yet another compromise for Dorothea, and therefore, yet another demonstration that Dorothea is well-nigh paralysed by the lack of opportunity presented to her. It is apt, however, to consider the other marriages mentioned in the Finale, alongside Dorothea's. Lydgate has been unable to combine his public ambitions and his private emotions, his career and his marriage, to

155

form a successful whole. In his case, the unhappiness and mismatch of himself and Rosamond prevent his wider endeavours:

he always regarded himself as a failure: he had not done what he once meant to do . . . He once called her his basil plant; and when she asked for an explanation, said that basil was a plant which had flourished wonderfully on a murdered man's brains. Rosamond had a placid but strong answer to such speeches. Why then had he chosen her? (p. 893)

This glimpse of the Lydgates' later married life tells us that despite Lydgate's acceptance of his burden, there has been no forgiveness or genuine reconciliation. The failure of a marriage between two such promising and trained individuals leaves the ending of the novel open in a general way. The question of what makes a happy marriage – so compelling an image for George Eliot – is never resolved. Fred and Mary Vincy, and Sir James and Celia Chettam are happy. However, by remaining in Middlemarch they have been left behind in an historical backwater. Mary has educated Fred into the Middlemarch values of hard work and thrift. Sir James finds a compliant wife who appears to corroborate his early views of the relative powers of the sexes:

Sir James had no idea that he should ever like to put down the predominance of this handsome girl, in whose cleverness he delighted. Why not? A man's mind – what there is of it – has always the advantage of being masculine – as the smallest birch-tree is of a higher kind than the most soaring palm – and even his ignorance is of a sounder quality. Sir James might not have originated this estimate; but a kind Providence furnishes the limpest personality with a little gum or starch in the form of tradition. (pp. 43–4)

Later events demonstrate that Sir James, the great traditionalist, does *not* delight in clever women, and that he is better suited to the conventionally feminine and pliant Celia than to Dorothea. This restatement of the status quo in the final pages of the novel must be read alongside George Eliot's description of progress: 'that things are not so ill with you and me as they might have been, is half owing to the number who lived faithfully a hidden life, and rest in unvisited tombs' (p. 896). The paradoxes of failure and progress, success and compromise pervade the Finale, and the question of Dorothea's history remains unanswered.

Recent feminist critics have frequently discussed the topic of the woman writer. Do women write differently from men, or about different topics? More specifically, is George Eliot's writing a 'gendered' writing? The discussion focuses on two areas: her use of a male pseudonym, and the dominance in her fiction of a knowledgeable authorial voice.

There were many women writing under their own names in the 1840s and 1850s: for example, Mrs Gaskell, Geraldine Jewsbury and Charlotte Yonge. G. H. Lewes had even written several articles and reviews on the phenomenon of the woman novelist before he and Marian began to live together. The possible scandal attaching to the woman living with a married man was evidently one reason why the early novels appeared under a pseudonym. However, the adoption of a man's name was also a claim for a quasi-male authority, and for the serious attention accorded to men writers but not generally to women writers. In 'Silly Novels by Lady Novelists' (1856), significantly written just before George Eliot began to write fiction herself, she dissociates herself amusingly but intolerantly from the wealth of popular women's fiction being produced at the time. Like all articles in *The Westminster Review*, this appeared anonymously, thereby assuming a male voice:

Silly novels by Lady Novelists are a genus with many species, determined by the particular quality of silliness that predominates in them – the frothy, the prosy, the pious, or the pedantic. But it is a mixture of all these – a composite order of feminine fatuity, that produces the largest class of such novels, which we shall distinguish as the *mind-and-millinery* species.

Her greatest scorn, in fact, is reserved for those novels which parade a vain erudition:

the most mischievous form of feminine silliness is the literary form, because it tends to confirm the popular prejudice against the more solid education of women. When men see girls wasting their time in consultations about bonnets and ball dresses, and in giggling or sentimental love-confidences, or middle-aged women mismanaging their children, and solacing themselves with acrid gossip, they can hardly help saying, 'For heaven's sake, let girls be better educated; let them have some better objects of thought – some more solid occupations.' But after a few hours' conversation with an oracular literary woman, or a few hours' reading of her books, they are likely enough to say, 'After all, when a woman gets some knowledge, see what use she makes of it.'

This denotes an extreme refusal to identify herself with women who were, on the whole, struggling to attain learning. In attacking the foibles and failings of such women writers, George Eliot fails to confront patriarchal assumptions, and those social constraints which had partly caused women to write such nonsense. She requires of women, instead, a seriousness that should be judged equally with men's writing, for

if they are inclined to resent our plainness of speech, we ask them to reflect for a moment on the chary praise, and often captious blame, which their panegyrists give to writers whose works are on the way to become classics. No sooner does a woman show that she has genius or effective talent, than she receives the tribute of being moderately praised and severely criticised. By a peculiar thermometric adjustment, when a woman's talent is at zero, journalistic approbation is at the boiling pitch; when she attains mediocrity, it is already at no more than summer heat; and if ever she reaches excellence, critical enthusiasm drops to the freezing point. Harriet Martineau, Currer Bell, and Mrs Gaskell have been treated as cavalierly as if they had been men.

George Eliot's perception that most women writers are condescended to by reviewers is apt here, but her stipulation that women meet male standards is peremptory, and this peremptoriness is emphasized by the male authority implicit in the tone of the article.

George Eliot evidently enjoyed the anonymity of journalism, which allowed her to appear in print under the guise of a certain male authority. *Adam Bede* was published when the mystery surrounding the pseudonym, 'George Eliot', was at its height. In fact, Dickens was almost the only reader of the novel to feel certain that George Eliot was a woman, although some of her close friends felt that they recognized their friend Marian in the prose and the ideas. When the truth behind the pseudonym was revealed, and George Eliot became in the public's minds a woman writer, the effects were twofold. There was a predictable change of response in the reviews of her later novels, emphasis shifting from the intelligence and strength of the writer to the more 'feminine' qualities of feeling, sympathy and insight. It is also possible that certain authorial shifts in tone and concern may be discerned, in *The Mill on the Floss* and *Felix Holt*, for example: these include an increased interest in women's states of mind, feelings, education and personal dilemmas.

In *Middlemarch* George Eliot is writing at the height of her powers. What is notable about the authorial voice is its scope of knowledge, both about the characters, and about science, philosophy, history, medicine and scholarship. That very knowledge led contemporary women writers to contest that George Eliot wrote 'like a man'. And sexist assumptions about the abilities appropriate to each sex still prevail in some quarters. Writing in 1979, George Levine says,

Certainly, no novelist of the time could compete with her in sheer breadth of learning, or move so easily among Greek, Hebrew, and Italian literatures, or the most recent developments in science and philosophy, or art and music, or history, politics, sociology, law, and anthropology. Even now, it is easy to read George Eliot as a 'male' novelist.[17]

But Virginia Woolf was an early reader who perceived that the adoption of a pseudonym and of an authoritative voice might signify something more complex:

It may have been not only with a view to obtaining impartial criticism that George Eliot and Miss Brontë adopted male pseudonyms, but in order to free their own consciousness as they wrote from the tyranny of what was expected from their sex.[18]

Perhaps the scope 'degenders' the authorial voice to some extent – in the same way as 'George Eliot', by signifying Marian Lewes, erases gender distinctions. Jennifer Uglow calls *Middlemarch* a 'curiously sly, androgynous book – which illuminates with uncanny credibility the dark mental corners of both men and women', while Gillian Beer says that, in general, 'The writing allows us, through passionate inhabiting of diversity, to move outside the prescriptions of gender-roles with which, however various, we enter. It gives us intelligence.'

Both Uglow and Beer base their conclusions on the way in which the psychological insight displayed in *Middlemarch* applies equally to female and male characters. Indeed, the issue of the gender of an author is frequently focused on the presentation of characters. There was a lengthy debate when *Middlemarch* was published about whether George Eliot could create male characters or not, the received wisdom being that women writers could not depict men, while men writers comprehended women. Henry James, in his review of *Middlemarch*, said of Ladislaw, 'He is, we may say, the one figure which a masculine intellect of the same power as George Eliot's would not have conceived with the same complacency; he is, in short, roughly speaking, a woman's man.' (This recurred when Leslie Stephen said of the final novel, *Daniel Deronda*, 'One feels, I think, that Grandcourt was drawn by a woman.') In *Middlemarch*, just as Dorothea is portrayed sympathetically, so, on the whole, are Lydgate, Casaubon and even Bulstrode accorded considerable authorial insight, penetration and detailed investigation. The presentation of these characters leads many readers to attest that George Eliot *could* convincingly depict male characters. Interestingly, while Ladislaw, as we have seen, invariably invites criticism from reviewers and readers, some recent feminist criticism has recuperated him as a positive creation. In patriarchal terms, he is a failure, being sketched in somewhat idealistically by an author who is partial to the idea of him, and within the novel, being superficial and undirected. In feminist terms he represents, Sandra Gilbert and Susan Gubar suggest, 'Eliot's radically anti-patriarchal attempt to create an image of masculinity attractive to women.' His personality and situation carry qualities traditionally associated with women: emotion, impulse, dependency, and lack of financial power. But being a man in the society of the novel, he, unlike the female characters, is empowered to travel and to experiment with various occupations in his search for a vocation.

George Eliot's attitude towards women's causes of her time was complex and ambivalent. Many of her closest female friends in the 1850s and 1860s (closest perhaps because they were sufficiently broadminded still to visit her) were active in the women's movement: women such as Barbara Bodichon and Emily Davies. There were many lively areas of debate during this period. The situation of impoverished single gentlewomen, the plight of governesses, and the sweated labour of seamstresses, were all concerns during the 1840s. These were superseded in the 1850s and 1860s by agitation for improved educational opportunities for women, for increased fields of employment, and for legal reform in the areas of married women having some rights over their property, increased freedom to divorce, and most importantly, the right to vote. There was intense discussion and petitioning around these issues. For example, Barbara Bodichon's treatise, *Women and Work*, was published in *The Englishwoman's Journal* in 1857; during the passage of the 1867 Reform Bill there was vigorous petitioning for women's franchise. In 1869 John Stuart Mill published *The Subjection of Women*. The women's college that was to become Girton College, Cambridge, opened in Hitchin in 1869, and *The Women's Suffrage Journal* commenced in 1870. However, the modern reader should bear in mind that none of these crusades was wholly successful until years after the decade of the 1860s.

George Eliot gave her support to several causes, such as the effort to push a Married Women's Property Bill through Parliament in the late 1850s, and she subscribed to the foundation of Girton College. In 1867, for example, she wrote to Barbara Bodichon, 'the better Education of Women is one of the objects about which I have *no doubt*'. But she consistently refused to participate actively in a women's movement, or to be identified publicly with women's causes. Her essays and letters sporadically reveal reservations about the 'fitness' of women, as they currently laboured under disadvantages of education and opportunity, to assume the full rights of citizenship. In 1853 she had written to Mrs Peter Alfred Taylor, 'Enfranchisement of women only makes creeping progress; and that is best, for woman does not yet deserve a much better lot than man gives her.' Writing to Sara Hennell in 1867, she called Women's Suffrage 'an extremely doubtful good', and in 1869, to Mrs Nassau John Senior, she said:

There is no subject on which I am more inclined to hold my peace and learn, than on the 'Women Question'. It seems to me to overhang abysses, of which even prostitution is not the worst. Conclusions seem easy so long as we keep large blinkers on and look in the direction of our own private path.

But on one point I have a strong conviction, and I feel bound to act on it, so far as my retired way of life allows of public action. And that is, that women ought to have the same fund of truth placed within their reach as men have . . .

I have been made rather miserable lately by revelations about women, and have resolved to remain silent in my sense of helplessness.

George Eliot fixed upon education as the great necessity for women, and therefore tended to see other aims as premature. In the light of her own intellectual achievements, she might be criticized for expressing a certain disdain for those women who had not shown such application or enjoyed such opportunities. She identified her own skills and status with the world of men, and in becoming a well-read journalist and a successful novelist, she strove to be accepted by the male world of education, philosophy and power on its own patriarchal terms. She was not anxious to demand that the criteria for success be realigned to include women's achievements.

However, while Dorothea is no George Eliot, and her story in no way a story about the exceptional woman, there is a sense in which George Eliot, and *Middlemarch* as her greatest novel, proffer the positive image of women that feminist critics sometimes hanker after. Henry James wrote after her death:

To her own sex her memory, her example, will remain of the highest value; those of them for whom, the 'development' of women is the hope of the future ought to erect a monument to George Eliot. She helped on the cause more than any one, in proving how few limitations are of necessity implied in the feminine organism. She went so far that such a distance seems enough, and in her effort she sacrificed no tenderness, no grace. There is much talk to-day about things being 'open to women'; but George Eliot showed that there is nothing that is closed.

Notes

I Biographical and Historical Background: (pp. 1–20)

1. Haight, Gordon S., *George Eliot: A Biography*, Oxford, Oxford University Press, 1968, p. 42.
2. ibid., p. 76.
3. ibid., p.190.
4. ibid., p. 219.
5. ibid., p. 432.
6. ibid., p. 443.
7. ibid., p. 435.
8. Williams, Ioan, *The Realist Novel in England: A Study in Development*, London, Macmillan, 1974, p. 171.
9. Haight, Gordon S., ed., *George Eliot: Letters*, New Haven, Connecticut, Yale University Press, 1954, vol. 3, p. 227.

II Contexts for *Middlemarch*: (pp. 21–75)

1. Perkin, Harold, *The Origins of Modern English Society 1780–1880*, London, Routledge & Kegan Paul, 1969, pp. 3–4.
2. Ferris, Sumner, '*Middlemarch*, George Eliot's Masterpiece', in *From Jane Austen to Joseph Conrad*, ed. R. C. Rathburn and M. Steinmann, Minnesota, Minnesota University Press, 1957, p. 196.
3. Evans, E. J., *The Great Reform Act of 1832*, London, Methuen, 1983, p. 1.
4. Dover Wilson, John, Introduction to Matthew Arnold, *Culture and Anarchy*, Cambridge, Cambridge University Press, 1960, p. xxxiii.
5. Woolf, Virginia, 'George Eliot', in *Women and Writing*, ed. Michele Barrett, London, Women's Press, 1979, p. 156.
6. Quoted in Willey, Basil, *Nineteenth-Century Studies*, p. 204.
7. Mayhew, Henry, *Mayhew's Characters*, ed. P. Quennell, London, Spring Books, 1951, p. 299.
8. Quoted in Swinden, Patrick, ed., *George Eliot: Middlemarch*, pp. 60–68.
9. Schorer, Mark, 'The Structure of the Novel: Method, Metaphor and Mind', in *Middlemarch: Critical Approaches to the Novel*, ed. Barbara Hardy, London, Athlone Press, 1967, p. 12.
10. Hardy, Barbara, *The Novels of George Eliot: A Study in Form*, London, Athlone Press, 1959, p. 107.

III Commentary and Analysis: (pp. 77–161)

1. Hulcoop, John F., '"This Petty Medium": In the Middle of *Middlemarch*', in *George Eliot: A Centenary Tribute*, eds. Gordon S. Haight and Rosemary T. Vanarsdel, London, Macmillan, 1982, pp. 154, 161.

2. Lee, Alan J., *The Origins of the Popular Press 1855–1914*, London, Croom Helm, 1976, p. 105.

3. ibid., p. 28.

4. Suvin, Darko, 'The Social Addressees of Victorian Fiction', in *Literature and History*, vol. 8:1, Spring 1982, p. 17.

5. Oldfield, Derek, 'The Language of the Novel: The Character of Dorothea', in *Middlemarch: Critical Approaches to the Novel*, ed. Barbara Hardy, London, Athlone Press, 1967, p. 81.

6. Knoepflmacher, U.C., 'The "Metaphysics" of *Middlemarch*', in *The Nineteenth-Century Novel: Critical Essays and Documents*, ed. Arnold Kettle, London, Heinemann, 1972, pp. 222, 221.

7. Irwin, Michael, *Picturing: Description and Illusion in the Nineteenth-Century Novel*, London, Allen & Unwin, 1979, p. 14.

8. Lerner, Lawrence, 'Dorothea and the Theresa-Complex', in *George Eliot: Middlemarch*, ed. Patrick Swinden, London, Macmillan, 1972.

9. Miller, J. Hillis, 'Optic and Semiotic in *Middlemarch*', in *The Worlds of Victorian Fiction*, ed. J. H. Buckley, Harvard, Harvard University Press, 1975, p. 143.

10. ibid., p. 138.

11. Mason, Michael, '*Middlemarch* and Science: Problems of Life and Mind', *Review of English Studies*, 22, 1971, p. 151.

12. MacCabe, Colin, *James Joyce and the Revolution of the Word*, London, Macmillan, 1978, p. 15.

13. Boumelha, Penny, 'George Eliot and the End of Realism', in *Women Reading Women's Writing*, ed. Sue Roe, Brighton, Harvester, 1987, p. 21.

14. Austen, Zelda, 'Why Feminist Critics Are Angry with George Eliot', *College English*, vol. 37, No. 6, February, 1976, p. 549.

15. Blake, Kathleen, '*Middlemarch* and the Woman Question', *Nineteenth-Century Fiction*, vol. 31, 1976, p. 301.

16. Millet, Kate, *Sexual Politics*, London, Hart-Davis, 1971, p. 139.

17. Levine, George, 'Repression and Vocation in George Eliot: A Review Essay', *Women and Literature*, vol. 7, 1979, p. 3.

18. Woolf, Virginia, 'Women Novelists', in *Women and Writing*, ed. Michele Barrett, London, Women's Press, 1979, p. 70.

Select Bibliography

Biography

Haight, Gordon S., *George Eliot: A Biography*, Oxford, Oxford University Press, 1968.

Haight, Gordon S., ed., *George Eliot: Letters*, New Haven, Connecticut, Yale University Press, 1954.

Uglow, Jennifer, *George Eliot*, London, Virago, 1987.

Context and Background

Beer, Gillian, *Darwin's Plots: Evolutionary Narrative in Darwin, George Eliot and Nineteenth-Century Fiction*, London, Routledge & Kegan Paul, 1983.

Beer, Gillian, *George Eliot*, Brighton, Harvester, 1986.

Chapman, Raymond, *The Sense of the Past in Victorian Literature*, London, Croom Helm, 1986.

Cosslett, Tess, *The 'Scientific Movement' and Victorian Literature*, Brighton, Harvester, 1982.

Gilbert, Sandra M., and Gubar, Susan, *The Madwoman in the Attic: The Woman Writer and the Nineteenth-Century Literary Imagination*, New Haven, Connecticut, Yale University Press, 1979.

Jay, Elisabeth, *The Religion of the Heart: Anglican Evangelicalism and the Nineteenth-Century Novel*, Oxford, Oxford University Press, 1979.

Pinney, Thomas, ed., *Essays of George Eliot*, London, Routledge & Kegan Paul, 1963.

Shuttleworth, Sally, *George Eliot and Nineteenth-Century Science: The Make-Believe of a Beginning*, Cambridge, Cambridge University Press, 1984.

Willey, Basil, *Nineteenth-Century Studies: Coleridge to Matthew Arnold*, London, Chatto & Windus, 1964.

Williams, Raymond, *The Country and the City*, London, Chatto & Windus, 1973.

Critical Studies

Ashton, Rosemary, *George Eliot*, Oxford, Oxford University Press, 1983.

Beaty, Jerome, *'Middlemarch' from Notebook to Novel: A Study of George Eliot's Creative Method*, Champaign, Illinois, University of Illinois, 1960.

Carroll, David, ed., *George Eliot: The Critical Heritage*, London, Routledge & Kegan Paul, 1971.

Daiches, David, *George Eliot: Middlemarch*, London, Edward Arnold, 1963.

Dentith, Simon, *George Eliot*, Brighton, Harvester, 1986.

Garrett, Peter K., *The Victorian Multiplot Novel: Studies in Dialogical Form*, New Haven, Connecticut, Yale University Press, 1980.

Graver, Suzanne, *George Eliot and Community: A Study in Social Theory and Fictional Form*, Berkeley, California, University of California Press, 1984.

Harvey, W. J., *The Art of George Eliot*, London, Chatto & Windus, 1961.

Kettle, Arnold. *An Introduction to the English Novel*, vol. I, London, Hutchinson, 1951.

Leavis, F. R., *The Great Tradition*, London, Chatto & Windus, 1948.

Swinden, Patrick, ed., *George Eliot: Middlemarch*, London, Macmillan, 1972.

FOR THE BEST IN PAPERBACKS, LOOK FOR THE 🐧

In every corner of the world, on every subject under the sun, Penguin represents quality and variety – the very best in publishing today.

For complete information about books available from Penguin – including Pelicans, Puffins, Peregrines and Penguin Classics – and how to order them, write to us at the appropriate address below. Please note that for copyright reasons the selection of books varies from country to country.

In the United Kingdom: Please write to *Dept E.P., Penguin Books Ltd, Harmondsworth, Middlesex, UB7 0DA*

If you have any difficulty in obtaining a title, please send your order with the correct money, plus ten per cent for postage and packaging, to *PO Box No 11, West Drayton, Middlesex*

In the United States: Please write to *Dept BA, Penguin, 299 Murray Hill Parkway, East Rutherford, New Jersey 07073*

In Canada: Please write to *Penguin Books Canada Ltd, 2801 John Street, Markham, Ontario L3R 1B4*

In Australia: Please write to the *Marketing Department, Penguin Books Australia Ltd, P.O. Box 257, Ringwood, Victoria 3134*

In New Zealand: Please write to the *Marketing Department, Penguin Books (NZ) Ltd, Private Bag, Takapuna, Auckland 9*

In India: Please write to *Penguin Overseas Ltd, 706 Eros Apartments, 56 Nehru Place, New Delhi, 110019*

In Holland: Please write to *Penguin Books Nederland B.V., Postbus 195, NL–1380AD Weesp, Netherlands*

In Germany: Please write to *Penguin Books Ltd, Friedrichstrasse 10–12, D–6000 Frankfurt Main 1, Federal Republic of Germany*

In Spain: Please write to *Longman Penguin España, Calle San Nicolas 15, E–28013 Madrid, Spain*

In France: Please write to *Penguin Books Ltd, 39 Rue de Montmorency, F-75003, Paris, France*

In Japan: Please write to *Longman Penguin Japan Co Ltd, Yamaguchi Building, 2–12–9 Kanda Jimbocho, Chiyoda-Ku, Tokyo 101, Japan*

FOR THE BEST IN PAPERBACKS, LOOK FOR THE 🐧

PENGUIN CRITICAL STUDIES

Described by *The Times Educational Supplement* as 'admirable' and 'superb', Penguin Critical Studies is a specially developed series of critical essays on the major works of literature for use by students in universities, colleges and schools.

Titles published or in preparation:

Antony and Cleopatra	Kenneth Muir
As You Like It	Peter Reynolds
The Great Gatsby	Kathleen Parkinson
Jane Eyre	Susie Campbell
Mansfield Park	Isobel Armstrong
Return of the Native	J. Garver
Rosenkrantz and Guildenstern are Dead	Roger Sales
Shakespeare's History Plays	C. W. R. D. Moseley
The Tempest	Sandra Clark
Tennyson	Roger Ebbatson
A Winter's Tale	Christopher Hardman
The Miller's Tale	John Cunningham
The Waste Land	Stephen Coote
The Nun's Priest's Tale	Stephen Coote
King Lear	Kenneth Muir
Othello	Gāmini and Fenella Salgādo